CONTENTS

INTRODUCTION

Throughout much of 2002, I was fortunate enough to be involved with a major photographic assignment of Ireland's fish and fisheries. Whilst I'd always appreciated the huge amount of angling on offer in Ireland, I'd never totally realised its full potential before. Irish fishing, whether fly, coarse or sea, is all but unique in this modern day and age of ours. Why? Simply so much is yet unexploited and unexplored. Whichever your discipline, chances are that you'll be hunting totally wild fish that owe nothing to hatcheries or stocking policies. Moreover, if there's even only the modicum of explorer about you, then in Ireland it's easy to find virgin pike waters or small stream brown trout that have never seen a fly. And as for the sea fishing… there are probably more marks undreamt of even, than have yet been discovered.

Ireland was once described as 'the angler's Paradise in the west', and though things have inevitably changed, a large part of this description holds true. In some part, developments have even been for the better. Swift ferries now make the crossing a breeze. European money has transformed the country's road networks. Accommodation is much improved and more readily available since the 1960s. There's a Tourist Board that's uniquely well-staffed and totally geared up to the needs of anglers. Today, there is tackle and bait both readily available so, in short, you have the best of the old combined with the advantages of the new.

Above all, any trip to Ireland is the perfect way to restore batteries depleted by the pell-mell demands of modern life. The roads, though improved, are still quiet. The countryside remains uniquely peaceful. The landscape is breathtakingly unaltered. The Irish people are warm, welcoming and wickedly amusing. Obviously Shangri-Las do not exist, and Ireland has its problems with fish farms, poaching and over-intensive farming, but there is a mighty will in the country to remove these shadows and a multitude of successes are already shining through. Irish fishing will continue to improve. Believe me, the future's bright – and it's vivid emerald green.

JOHN BAILEY'S FISHING GUIDES

WHERE TO
FISH
IN IRELAND

JOHN BAILEY'S FISHING GUIDES

WHERE TO FISH IN IRELAND

FLY FISHING · COARSE FISHING · SEA FISHING

John Bailey

NEW HOLLAND

First published in 2003 by New Holland Publishers (UK) Ltd
London • Cape Town • Sydney • Auckland

www.newhollandpublishers.com

2 4 6 8 10 9 7 5 3 1

Garfield House, 86–88 Edgware Road, London W2 2EA

80 McKenzie Street, Cape Town 8001, South Africa

14 Aquatic Drive, Frenchs Forest, NSW 2086, Australia

218 Lake Road, Northcote, Auckland, New Zealand

ISBN 1 84330 558 5

Publishing Manager: Jo Hemmings
Senior Editor: Kate Michell
Assistant Editor: Rose Hudson
Design: Gülen Shevki
Concept Designer: Andrew Easton
Production Controller: Joan Woodroffe

Index by Indexing Specialists,
202 Church Road, Hove BN3 2DJ

Reproduction by Pica Digital Pte Ltd, Singapore
Printed and bound in Singapore by Kyodo Printing Co. (Singapore) Pte Ltd

The publishers' numbering system in Ireland is subject to change. Whilst every
effort for accuracy was made whilst going to press, some of the numbers
published in this book may be affected by these changes. Should you encounter
difficulties, if in Ireland, dial 1190 and if in the UK and that you dial 11 8 11 for

MAP OF IRELAND

WHERE TO
FLY FISH
IN IRELAND

FLY-FISHING SITES IN IRELAND

1 Lough Corrib
2 Inagh Lodge
3 Ballynahinch
4 Delphi Lodge
5 Lough Mask
6 Lough Carra
7 Loughs Conn & Cullin
8 River Moy
9 Lough Arrow
10 Lough Melvin
11 Knockbracken
12 The Sperrins
13 Glenowen
14 Straid Trout Fishery
15 Lough Ennell
16 Aughrim Trout Fishery
17 River Mulcair
18 Ballyvolane House &
River Blackwater
19 Lough Currane
20 Glencar

It's sad but true that when many anglers from across the seas think of Ireland they concentrate on south of the border. Of course, there is superb fishing there, but I urge you to reconsider what the north has to offer. In fact, my own belief is – and I've seen virtually every water in all of the island – that the north can offer every bit as much as the south. We've got some fabulous salmon runs, you can pick up sea trout in all manner of unexpected places and some of our brown trout fishing is beyond compare. What's more, most of it – or at least much of it – is one big, well-kept secret. Everybody knows about the big southern loughs, Mask, Corrib and Conn, but we've got waters that would make any southerner sit up!

MIKE SHORTT, IRISH WRITER, CELEBRITY AND ADVISOR

TO THE NORTHERN IRISH TOURIST BOARD

There you have it. Ireland – whether north or south of the border – is a place teeming with opportunities for the fly fisherman. There's unprecedented wild fishing but, at the same time, there are the more intimate, commercial fisheries where you can build up your confidence! But then, Ireland is more than just about fishing alone. The countryside – so green, clean and uncluttered. The roads – often so empty you'd think yourself back in the 1930s. Sleepy villages. Welcoming bars, and, inevitably, a pint of Guinness waiting. In fact, for the fisherman, most of the business is done in the bars. If you want to know anything, go into the bar, ask around and you will get to hear where there is a boat to hire, a ghillie willing to turn out or when you can expect the next hatch of sedges!

LOUGH CORRIB – CO. GALWAY

Corrib, in the west of Ireland, is truly a trout fisherman's paradise. It is over thirty miles long and covers some forty-four thousand acres, liberally scattered with islands and endowed with endless amounts of stunning fish! The lake varies greatly from one area to the next. In lower Corrib, for example, the water is generally quite shallow with depths averaging six to ten feet. The water here is very clear and weedy and there's an abundance of fly life. The northern end of the lake has many shallows too, but also has areas as deep as a hundred and fifty feet. These chasms are also of great interest to the fisherman as they hold many brown trout, including ferox trout, some weighing over fifteen pounds.

Corrib as a whole is a limestone lake and is rich in feeding. Indeed, trout are caught by fly fishermen as early as February, even fishing in the shallows with floating lines and teams of wet flies and nymphs. In March and April, local anglers wait eagerly, however, for the Duck fly. This is a chironamid, black in colour with white wings, and it appears in weedy areas in great numbers. The trout gorge themselves, especially feasting on the pupae. April can also be a good month with good hatches of olives all over the lake. But the real attraction comes when the mayfly appears. From early May, right into June, this magical period sees many visitors on the Corrib as people flock from far and wide. Wet-fly fishing, dapped naturals and dry-fly fishing are all successful. The middle and top half of the lake fish best, particularly around Oughterhard and Greenfields. With a lull in July, August and September can fish well. Sedge patterns and wet flies take a large share of the catches.

Let's have a chat about the ferox... these fish, as I've already said, are usually taken in the northern end of the lake and Inchagoill island is a famous area to work. They feed heavily on roach, small trout and char here. Trolled baits work well in the twenty- to thirty-foot band. Always, however, be careful of bottom contours when trolling. Corrib, like all these western loughs, can throw up reefs and shoals when you least expect them so keep a close look out and never travel too fast over unfamiliar water.

SEASON – the fly-fishing season runs from 15th February until 30th September.

TICKETS – The trout fishing is free on Corrib but a salmon licence is required. Many hotels issue licences. Alternatively, contact boatmen. Michael Ryan at River Lodge, Cong, County Mayo, on 00353 (0)92 46057, is very knowledgeable, and also rents out boats. Also try Michael Walsh, Ower Guesthouse, Greenfields, Headford, County Galway on 00353 (0)93 35446. The tackle shop in Clonbur on 00353 (0)92 46197 is a fund of information.

DIRECTIONS – Corrib, with its huge size, is really hard to miss. Situated just north of Galway, it is well served by roads both east and west.

ACCOMMODATION – Highly recommended is the idyllic Currarevagh House in Oughterard, County Galway, which has its own fishing facilities. Contact Harry and June Hodgson on 00353 (0)91 552313. Alternatively, phone the Galway Tourist Information Office on 00353 (0)91 563081, or Basil Shiels at Ardnassillagh Lodge, Oughterard, on 00353 (0)91 552550.

BALLYNAHINCH AND INAGH LODGE – CO. GALWAY

If you want to experience some of the grandest, wildest, most traditional fishing that Connemara has to offer then these two splendid fishing houses ought to be your target. Both are situated on the Ballynahinch river system, Inagh a few miles upstream. And both come with a remarkable fishing history.

Ballynahinch is like something out of a Hollywood set or a Gothic novel: a magnificent castle appearing from woodlands, overlooking the enchanting river. Its fishing has been legendary for decades and during the 1920s and 1930s it became the spiritual home of His Highness the Maharaja Jam Sahib of Nawanagar, the sporting prince better known as Ranji. He'd probably recognise the river today even after sixty or seventy years, but he would be disappointed by the numbers of sea trout. Fish farms have had their effect, of course, but the news is promising. Numbers of sea trout are on the increase and wise angling policies appear to be taking their effect.

Inagh Lodge is more remote, more starkly situated but offers equally magnificent fishing for both sea trout and spring and summer salmon fishing. Inagh offers two outstanding loughs: Inagh itself and Derryclare. These are both hauntingly beautiful and fish well for sea trout, salmon and an increasing number of large browns which are now frequently topping the five-pound barrier.

Daytime sea trout fishing is now an Inagh speciality: approach the pools with extreme caution, fish upstream to rising fish with tiny dry flies and expect fireworks.

SEASON – The salmon season opens officially on 1st February and extends to 30th September, though the effective season begins in late March with spring salmon running through to May. Grilse start running around mid-May, with the river in top form through June and July. The sea trout begin running in late June or early July and stocks are augmented throughout August and September by the smaller sea trout known as finnock or harvesters.

TICKETS – It is required by law to have a licence to fish for salmon and sea trout, and these can be purchased on arrival at both fisheries.

ACCOMMODATION AND DIRECTIONS – The address of both fishing houses is Recess, Connemara, and they are reached most commonly by the N59 from Galway. Continue through Maamcross and turn right at Recess for Inagh and carry on towards Clifden for Ballynahinch which you will find on the left. For Ballynahinch, telephone 00353 (0)95 31006 or email bhincb@iol.ie For Inagh telephone 00353 (0)95 34706 or email Inagh@iol.ie

DELPHI LODGE – CO. GALWAY

I first made my way to Delphi Lodge in the summer of 2002 and wondered for the life of me why I hadn't travelled there earlier. The Lodge, built in the 1830s, is elegant, comfortable and welcoming. The landscape is quite fabulous, other-

worldly, remarkable even in a country as breathtaking as Ireland. And the fishing is just extraordinary. What is also extraordinary is the effort that Peter Mantle, the owner, has put into saving the fishery. Not so long ago, Delphi was one of the most famous sea trout fisheries on earth. Enter the fish farms. Exit the sea trout. Rather than let Delphi perish, Peter Mantle instituted a fish farm and a pioneering scheme of salmon smolt release. The effect has been galvanizing: Delphi is now up and running again, this time delighting visitors with the number and quality of the salmon. As Peter freely admits, this is not the Delphi of old but it's a fine example of how man and nature can work in harmony to repair at least some of the damage done.

The lakes surrounding Delphi are stunning, with a magical atmosphere. For me, though, the Bundorragha River is the real thrill of the fishery. It's exactly my sort of river: comparatively small, dotted with entertaining pools, crystal clear so that sight fishing is quite possible. This is cautious, creepy-crawly stuff and long casting is rarely necessary or even desirable. Far better to put a fly down delicately and work it exactly where you know the fish are lying. Delphi now has salmon running pretty well throughout the season; a remarkable testimony to the skill, foresight and dedication of Peter Mantle and his team. This is a fishery reborn that is hugely worth a visit.

SEASON – The salmon season runs from 1st February to 30th September. Sea trout runs from 1st July to 30th September. Note that all wild salmon and all trout must be returned alive. Tagged salmon, however, must be killed. These rules are for the absolute good of the fish stocks.

TICKETS – A state licence is necessary for salmon and sea trout. Permits are issued at the hotel and rates depend on the time of the year.

ACCOMMODATION – Delphi Lodge has twelve rooms. Telephone 00353 (0)95 42222. Email info@delphilodge.ie

DIRECTIONS – It's not that Delphi Lodge is difficult to find, exactly – it's just that it's very remote. Find Leenane on the N59 and ask detailed directions from the village. Delphi is a local institution so there should be no problems.

LOUGH MASK – CO. GALWAY

Lough Mask is a limestone lake of twenty-two thousand acres. Perch, eels, char, huge pike and probably some of the very best brown trout fishing in Europe. Possibly one of the best months of my life was spent fishing Lough Mask in 1991. I admit that at the time I was primarily trolling for ferox trout: up until then, I probably caught about a dozen in as many years of trying in Scotland. In that one month, I boated forty ferox trout between five and ten pounds.

Since then, I've been back principally with a fly rod, but the dream has continued. I just love Mask anyway. The softly enchanting west of Ireland. The villages and towns.

The people. The lough islands where you can stop and brew a cup of heavenly-tasting tea. The mountains in the mists. And the wonderful trout fishing. They say that the mayfly season between mid-May and mid-June cannot be bettered, but I've enjoyed exhilarating days with daddy longlegs and grasshopper patterns way into September. Yes, dapping is a large part of what Mask is about and if you haven't tried it yet I urge you to get out with a boatman and learn this most fascinating and satisfying skill.

Of course, you can catch Lough Mask trout as you would on any Scottish loch or English reservoir, simply drifting, working teams of wet flies. This is blissful enough but, I repeat, do try the dap between mid-May and the end of summer if you can.

The beauty of Lough Mask trout deserves a special emphasis. These are absolutely pristine, wild brown trout and, excitingly, they probably average around about the one-and-a-half-pound mark. Certainly four- and five-pound fish are common. And talking about brown trout, let's mention Lough Carra – an offshoot of Mask, a bay almost, but at four thousand acres, a serious water in its own right. Shallow and extraordinarily fertile, Lough Carra produces browns that are probably the pick of a very exotic bunch.

Mask, especially as the sun goes down on a gentle-breezed day, is close to magic.

SEASON – early and late fly fishing in March and October can prove difficult and the very best of it really begins in May and runs through to mid-September.

PERMISSION – the fishing on Mask is free but it makes sense to join one of the local angling clubs for an outlay of £5 or so. Ballinrobe, Cong and Tourmakready all have their own associations, and they will help the visitor immensely with all manner of local knowledge and advice. They can also issue maps to show you the best access points.

BOAT HIRE – to get the very best out of Mask, you either need to take your own boat or hire one. Cushlough is a good centre for boat hire, as is the bay of Islands Park and Cahir Pier. On Carra, try Robert's Angling Service on 00353 (0)92 43046. Mr R. O'Grady of Ballinrobe on 00353 (0)92 41142 also has boats for hire.

DIRECTIONS – Lough Mask is situated off the N84, between Castlebar and Ballinrobe.

ACCOMMODATION – all the towns around Mask have numerous small hotels and bed and breakfast facilities. Robert's Angling Service also operates a guesthouse for anglers. Also try Ard Aoidhinn Angling Centre on 00353 (0)92 44009 and Derry Park Lodge Angling Centre on 00353 (0)92 44081. You will find warm hospitality from everyone in Mask.

LOUGHS CONN AND CULLIN – CO. MAYO

Conn is often overshadowed by its illustrious neighbours Mask and Corrib, but it shouldn't be. This is a stunningly beautiful, tranquil area and both Conn and its smaller partner, Cullin, nestle into the mountain scenery wonderfully well. The trout fishing remains of the highest quality and is likely to improve as domestic sewage and agricultural run-off problems are brought under control. Conn has a remarkable mayfly season when fishing can be wondrous, with

browns averaging two pounds or more. Cullin is at its best early season, as it's a shallow, rich lough and excessive weed can be a problem during the high summer months.

For both loughs, the peak of the summer can see slow fishing but Conn especially comes on again strongly towards the end of the season. But trout aren't the only attraction on Conn: spring salmon enter at the end of March and throughout April, and an often prolific grilse run starts in May and continues well into the summer months. The salmon are found over well-defined areas and frequently are very numerous. Look for drifts over fine sand and stony bottoms where the water averages some six-feet or so. But best of all, link up with one of the many expert boatmen in the area.

I personally can't think of a better base than Healy's Hotel in Pontoon, just out of Foxford. This really is a fisherman's inn based on the shores of Cullin with its own small fishing fleet. Graham Williams, one of the (admittedly English) guides there, knows the area inside out. And even if you don't actually catch a fish you can be guaranteed a riotous time. This man wasn't director of the satirical programme *Spitting Image* for many years without imbibing its scurrilous sense of humour!

Treating yourself to a boatman makes huge common sense if you've already made the investment of a long journey to the west of Ireland. Not only will your pleasure in the day be enhanced but your knowledge will come forward in leaps and bounds. There's also the safety aspect: Conn's water level rises and falls with rapidity and not all the dangerous clusters of rocks are marked adequately. Be warned.

SEASON – Trout runs from 15th February until 10th October, though most fishing begins in mid-March. Salmon fishing runs from 1st February to 30th September.

TICKETS – A permit is not required to fish Conn or Cullin but anglers are encouraged to purchase share certificates from the North-western Fisheries Co-operative Society whose function is to raise funds for fisheries development in the region. Remember that a state licence is required by law for salmon fishing. These licences can be obtained from most tackle shops and hotels as well as the Fisheries Board.

DIRECTIONS – Conn and Cullin are hard to miss! From Foxford take the R318 westwards towards Pontoon. There are a number of access points along this road. Healy's Hotel will be found on the junction with the 310 tucked away by a corner of Lough Cullin. To the north Crossmolina is another popular access point and boats can be launched from Gortnorabbey Pier.

ACCOMMODATION – Healy's Hotel, Pontoon, Foxford, County Mayo is particularly recommended. Telephone 00353 (0)94 9256443. Email: info@healyspontoon.com

THE RIVER MOY – CO. MAYO

It is obviously important to include the Moy here, as it is the river system that feeds the salmon into Loughs Conn and Cullin. The Moy system is extraordinarily prolific, and though the river itself is only sixty-odd miles long, the endless streams and tributaries make up a vast catchment area. To be honest, much of the Moy is not particularly suitable for fly fishing and the long, deep, slow-moving pools are best attacked with spinner and bait. However, there are huge exceptions to what is a very shaky rule.

Let's look at the estuary first, which teems with sea trout and is only really coming to be exploited by fly fishermen. Fishing can be done from the bank but boats are probably more reliable. Local experts, like Jud Ruane, have in recent years made important leaps forward in this really exciting form of fishing.

And then, inevitably, we come to the Moy Fishery in Ballina, probably one of the most famous salmon angling venues in the world, where it's not unusual to have annual catches of over five thousand fish. But fishing at Ballina is a real spectacle and it's not for you if you're of the shy, retiring kind who likes only cows or crows for company. In fact, in Ballina angling is the major spectator sport. Fish the Ridge Pool or the Cathedral Beat for example and you're likely to have an audience of scores if the river is right and fish are to be expected. And, when the river is good, it can be absolutely phenomenal.

The Moy isn't only about Ballina. The Mount Falcon Fisheries, the Attymass Fisheries, the Knockmore Fisheries, Byrne's, Armstrong's, Gannon's, Baker's, Cloongee and Ballintemple upstream are all prolific fisheries that have enchanted anglers.

Many locals use nine- or ten-foot single-handed rods, often in conjunction with trout flies as small as size sixteen. Don't neglect mayfly patterns either, but probably favourite are shrimp patterns along with the Hairy Mary, the Blue Charm, the Stoat's Tail and the Sabas Fry. You can be sure that local advice will be plentiful.

The Moy might not be everybody's idea of the classic salmon river but it's extraordinarily prolific and hugely characterful. If you're a serious salmon fan, a trip to Ireland wouldn't be quite complete without a visit.

SEASON – Salmon runs from 1st February until 30th September, sea trout from 1st February to 10th October and brown trout from 15th February until 10th October.

TICKETS – All anglers fishing for salmon or sea trout must be in possession of a valid state licence. These can be purchased from tackle shops and a range of other outlets. In addition, a permit from the fishery owner is normally required in order to fish for salmon and/or sea trout. Details of fishery owners on the Moy system are easily available from the tackle shops in Ballina. Try the Ridge Pool Bar on Bridge Street, telephone 00353 (0)96 21150. Further upstream, Jones' of Foxford on 00353 (0)94 56121 have information on the river thereabouts.

DIRECTIONS – Ballina, the gateway to the Moy is situated on the N26 north of Castlebar and west of Sligo.

CONTACTS – Jud Ruane at the Riverboat Inn, Ballina is a mine of information particularly on the estuarial fishing. Contact him on 00353 (0)96 22183.

ACCOMMODATION – Try the Foxford Lodge which prides itself on its fishing-friendly attitude. Telephone 00353 (0)94 57777.

LOUGH ARROW – BRICKLIEVE MOUNTAINS – CO. SLIGO

Lough Arrow is unique. The Bricklieve Mountains rise to the west of the lake and as the sun sets, ancient burial mounds are silhouetted in this most lost and wondrous of Irish landscapes. Lough Arrow is one of the unsung Irish heroes – over three thousand acres, spring-fed from under limestone streams. With no population or pollution to ruin its natural balance, it is home to wide-ranging fly hatch. Like many of the western loughs, Arrow is a haven for the mayfly: fish artificials or catch the real mayfly and use them on a blow line. This is when the really big wild browns can be caught and beautiful specimens are landed.

Buzzer fishing in May can be excellent whilst July and August sees two large sedge hatches – the great red sedge and the green Peter sedge. Dense flies often cloud round the boat like a mist. This provides great evening fishing and during the thirty minutes or so of the rise, the water can really look as though it's on the boil. By September, life is beginning to slow down and most of the locals go back on traditional wet flies.

There are many hotspots on this intriguing water. Look for areas around islands and reed beds. During the mayfly season, head for those areas of the shore that are tree-lined. Arrow is famous for its pristine, large browns. Two pounds is average, and threes and fours come out regularly, with the odd five-pounder thrown in. But how these fish fight! In the deep, crystal water these browns with majestic tails give any fisherman a time to remember.

SEASON – trout fishing runs from April to October.

TICKETS – you can't really do better for either tickets or boat hire than contacting Robert Maloney at Arrow Lodge, Kilmactranny, via Boyle, County Sligo, on 00353 (0)79 66298.

DIRECTIONS – Lough Arrow is in the north-west of Southern Ireland, just to the north of Boyle. Approach it on the N4 from the town.

ACCOMMODATION – Robert and Stephanie Maloney run the aptly named Arrow Lodge right on the shores of the lough. I cannot recommend this too highly. The Lodge was built for fishermen nearly two centuries ago and rejoices in its current role. Comfortable, on the waterside and with the most knowledgeable of local ghillies, at the very least phone Robert for all the information you need on this fascinating water.

LOUGH MELVIN – CO. LEITRIM/DONEGAL

Lough Melvin is a truly wonderful water, straddling the border between North and South, half in Leitrim, half in Donegal. A beautiful water indeed and a famous one for many reasons, in part because of its fish stocks. Lough Melvin has happy memories for me: I was a member of a party fishing there in March 2000 when Fred Buller, the famous fly fisherman and pike historian, caught one of the fabulously rare sonaghan trout for which Melvin is justifiably famous.

This was an important moment: Buller had, by catching it, almost completed a full house! Yes, he'd caught all but one of every British freshwater fish species that swims... I believe the missing member is a vendace.

A sonaghan is recognisable by its colour, size, shoaling habits and huge tail. They average between three quarters of a pound and a pound and a quarter and they're dark in colour – a sort of gunmetal silver. That great big tail, quite distinctive, means that they fight frenetically, often with extraordinary leaps into the air. They tend to shoal down deep where they feed on daphnia. Small flies, therefore, frequently pick them up and when you get one, you'll generally get others.

Then we come to another Melvin speciality – the gillaroos. Once again, these aren't huge fish, generally between a pound and a pound and a quarter, but what they lack in size is over-compensated for by staggering beauty. They are plastered with the most extraordinary, massive red spots. Catch them mainly in the shallows on dark flies on rough days. Gillaroos are primarily snail feeders, searching for them in the shallows.

Melvin isn't done yet – brown trout, char, ferox trout, salmon and grilse... a heady combination. Spring can be slow, but as soon as the weather warms, the lake comes alive. In early spring, most people are out trolling for salmon that come up the River Drowse. From April, though, the trout fishing takes off. Late June onwards sees the mayfly hatch. As summer progresses, the grilse really begin to take over and you can catch those easily dapping with the mayfly. Look for the grilse, especially, around Laureen Bay and Rossinver Bay – two places much favoured by the locals. You can still troll, of course, and hope to pick up one of the ferox. These are magnificent beasts, perhaps not as large as those that you'll find in Mask and Corrib, but still impressive.

Do you go it alone or do you enjoy the company of one of Ireland's renowned ghillies? I would keenly recommend the latter. Melvin is a big water, and it pays you to use some short cuts. Moreover, these men are often a delight – full of stories and tips.

SEASON – the salmon fishing opens on 1st February and the trout on 1st March. Fishing ends on 30th September.

TICKETS – at present there is no limit on the number of day tickets that are available at £10 per rod per day or £25 per rod per season. You can buy tickets from Sean Maguire at Melvin Tackle in Garrison on 028 6865 8194. Failing that, both the Melvin Bar and the Riverside Bar in Garrison also stock tickets. Sean Maguire can also arrange a boatman. Also contact Thomas Gallagher, Kin Lough, County Leitrim for a boat on 00353 (0)72 41208. He has a huge knowledge of the lough and also controls fishing on the River Drowse.

DIRECTIONS – Lough Melvin straddles the border a few miles south of Ballyshannon. Garrison is situated on the B52, at the south-eastern end of the water.

CONTACTS: – Jim Dillon of Gillaroo Lodge, West End, Bundoran, County Donegal, is an able guide to Lough Melvin. Call him on 00353 (0)72 42357 or fax 00353 (0)72 42172.

ACCOMMODATION – there is a huge amount of bed and breakfast and hotel accommodation locally. Mrs Flannagan at Lake View House offers an excellent bed and breakfast. Phone her on 028 6865 8444. Mr Ferguson, on 01365 658743, offers self-catering accommodation at Devenish Villa Holiday Homes. You can even camp at the Lough Melvin Holiday Centre for £6 a night! Phone 028 6865 8142 for details.

KNOCKBRACKEN – CO. FERMANAGH

An interesting adventure this – a small commercial water in an area absolutely riddled with tremendous wild brown trout fishing. How on earth can you ever expect such a place to work? Well, the fact is that it does and the reasons are comparatively easy to see. Even if most of us purists would agree that wild fishing is the thing, it's still an inescapable fact that it can be moody. The big, wild loughs are either on or they're off, and fishing can be very much boom or bust. There are days when all of us just want a bend in our rod and that's where somewhere like Knockbracken fits the bill exactly.

And, as you'd expect in Ireland, Knockbracken is a beautiful venue, expertly tended, too. All fish must be killed, but just a few pounds gets you fishing and if you want to take your fish, you can get them expertly prepared back at the lodge. There is an any-method lake – super if you've got a family with you, of course – but the main lake is fly only, deep and clear. There are plenty of small fish in the margins and you'll often see big rainbows roaring in for the kill. Big, fit fish that fight like dervishes. All the usual techniques work, however. Buzzers do very well, along with dry flies and weighted nymphs and shrimps. In short, it's a great place where you know you can expect some action and that could be just what you need after a few days out on Lough Erne when the heavens have been throwing everything they've got at you!

SEASON – open all year.

TICKETS – £3.50 for adults, £2.50 for juniors. 70p per fish caught – these must be killed. £1.50 per pound to take away. Contact Knockbracken Trout Lakes, Trillick Road, Ballinamallard, County Fermanagh, Northern Ireland on 028 6638 8548.

DIRECTIONS – from Enniskillen, take the A32 north and then turn off on the B46, signposted Ballinamallard and Omagh. Go through Ballinamallard, heading north. The fishery entrance is on the left in about half a mile.

ACCOMMODATION – phone Enniskillen Tourist Information on 028 6632 3110.

THE SPERRINS – ULSTER

I was absolutely knocked out by the Sperrins on a recent visit. This is an impressive mountain range stretching from Donegal in the west to Lough Neagh in the east, the heart and the hub of Ulster. The four main towns of the region are Cookstown, Magherafelt, Omagh and Strabane. This is an area of outstanding natural beauty and, in many places, as lonely as any other area

of Ireland. The three major species are salmon, brown trout and sea trout, although you might also come across the dollaghan, a unique species of Lough Neagh migratory brown trout. These tend to be caught when they run the many tributaries from mid July to the end of October. They can average as much as two pounds and grow to over six pounds abnormally. They travel a long way before spawning, rather like salmon and sea trout. Fascinating fish.

The Sperrins offer tremendous salmon opportunities, especially along the Foyle system. The main tributaries running through the Sperrin region from the Foyle are the Mourne, Derg and Strule: fast-flowing rocky rivers. Salmon begin to enter them from April through to October. Then you've got the Owenkilleu and Glenelly rivers – classic spate rivers that fish very well in the summer and autumn. The Camowen and Owenreagh rivers also provide excellent backend fishing – often for grilse as well.

There are all sorts of surprises: to the north of the region, surrounded by mountains in the most awe-inspiring landscape, you'll find Moor Lough and Lough Ash – two waters both around thirty acres in extent and offering some classic wild brown trout fishing. On and on it goes – the Strule river, the Burn Dennet river... all marvellous waters, all set in stunning, wild countryside. Now that the troubles and the violence are so obviously on the decrease, Northern Ireland is increasingly offering a great deal to the visiting angler. There are tremendous possibilities across this beautiful country, but the Sperrins certainly are a jewel in a very considerable crown.

SEASON – the season in general runs from 1st April to 20th October.

TICKETS – for the salmon fishing on the Foyle rivers, contact the Foyle Fisheries Commission, 8 Victoria Road, Derry, BT47 2AB, on 028 7134 2100. For fishing in the Lough Neagh system, contact the Fisheries Conservation Board, 1 Mahon Road, Portadown, Craigavon, County Armagh, BT62 3EE, on 028 3833 4666. For Loughs Moor and Ash, contact the Fisheries Conservation Board as above. David Campbell at the Tackle Shop, 28 Main Street, Newtownstewart, on 028 8166 1543 can provide tickets for the River Mourne, the River Strule and the Glenelly River. Also contact him for the Camowen River, the Drumragh River and the Owenragh River. Chism Fishing Tackle, 25 Old Market Place, Omagh, on 028 8224 4932, is also a fund of information.

→ DIRECTIONS – the Omagh Tourist Information Centre, 1 Market Street, Omagh BBT78 1EE on 028 8224 7831 will issue a detailed map of the Sperrins area.

⊢ ACCOMMODATION –contact the Omagh Tourist Information Centre as above. Strabane Tourist Information Centre on 028 7188 3735, Cookstown Tourist Information on 028 8676 6727 and Magherafelt Tourist Information on 028 7963 1510 will also give details.

GLENOWEN – DERRY

Glenowen is a brave project and a very necessary one too for Derry, Northern Ireland's second city. If you find yourself here, you don't have to go far to find some very pleasing fishing. The fishery extends to nine or ten acres – a reservoir amidst twenty or so acres of public park situated close to the city's boundary. An unlikely place perhaps, but it is beautifully tended, attractive and gives you the feeling of being way out in the countryside. It's a government funded, co-operative exercise and one that is obviously working very well indeed. The water is clear, quite deep and the trout are in excellent condition.

You'll find some friendly locals on the water, more than willing to give advice and perhaps lend a fly or two. Above all, what makes this such a heart-warming place is the number of children that come here to learn. We all know that Ireland – north and south – is a wild fish paradise, but the fly-fishing can be difficult if conditions are against you. Hard for a child. Far better to work up his or her enthusiasm on a water like this. An attractive, safe, accessible water where fish aren't impossible to catch.

There are some good fish here – the fishery record is well into double figures – and they come to all manner of flies. In the deep water, however, it's not a bad idea to fish an intermediate line with lures or use a long leader and go for an imitative pattern. The fish will come up to the surface, so have a selection of buzzers and dries with you.

In short, it's great place to stop off if you're visiting. The family can be busy in Derry – increasingly a thriving city – while you get a bit of peace and quiet. Or, have just a couple of hours fishing whilst the family roam the very attractive parkland.

SEASON – open all year.

TICKETS – contact Glenowen Fishery, Westway, The Rath, Creggan Estate, Derry City on 028 7137 1544. A two fish limit plus catch and release is £11. A five-fish limit plus catch and release is £16. Junior tickets cost £6 and allow two fish to be taken.

DIRECTIONS – you need to get onto the west side of the city. Turn left off the Craigavon Bridge and turn right at the next mini-roundabout, which will be signposted for Carmelite Fathers. After about a hundred yards, turn left and go up a steep hill. Take the left at the T-junction by St Peter's School. After about a mile you will come to Creggan Country Park where you will find the fishery signposted. It is well known in the area.

ACCOMMODATION – contact Derry Tourist Information on 028 7126 7284.

STRAID TROUT FISHERY – CO. ANTRIM

Straid fishery fulfils a very important function, situated as it is a few miles from Belfast. It's a beautiful water, surrounded by fields and woodland. It's large, too, at twenty-two acres, and well stocked with rainbows. Average depth is between six and a half and seven feet, with occasional pockets going down to twelve. Water visibility is generally very good, it only really colours up after heavy rains.

Straid is popular for a number of reasons. Firstly, the size of the fish averages a healthy two pounds and they fight tremendously well. Secondly, stocking policies achieve just about the right balance. The water isn't too easy but not too difficult either, a perfect challenge for all. The ticket options also appeal greatly. There's a whole range of different prices so that anyone who just wants to come and fish for a couple of hours or so is well catered for. Parents and children will find the ticket to suit them.

All the usual methods work well on the water and you'll find that the lake has a good sedge hatch with large numbers of buzzers, midges and olives. So the trout are well fed and used to looking for imitative patterns. Wet flies on an intermediate line prove a popular combination – try Green Peter, Silver Invicta or Hare's Ear. Buzzers are particularly effective throughout the summer, fished deep or in the surface film. Imitative patterns – shrimps, beetles and so on – can be fished on a floating line on a long leader, and watch for very careful takes.

SEASON – open all year round.

TICKETS – contact Straid Trout Fishery, Ballymure, Nr. Ballyclare, County Antrim, on 028 9334 0099. There is a whole range of ticket options available. For example, catch and release tickets cost £10, and the two-fish bag limit at £11 is very popular. A five-fish limit costs £16 and junior tickets are also available from as little as £6. Boats are also available at a modest cost and tuition is also offered.

DIRECTIONS – take the M2 north from Belfast and turn off at junction 4, signposted Larne. Travel through to the village of Ballymure and take the second right, signposted Straid.

ACCOMMODATION – contact the Belfast Tourist Information Centre on 028 9024 6609.

LOUGH ENNELL – CO. WESTMEATH

Lough Ennell is a fabulous water and no more than an hour's drive from Dublin itself. It's famous for holding the Irish record trout, way back in 1884, which weighed in at 26lb 2oz. Ennell isn't considered a huge lough by Irish standards – it's only six or seven miles long! It is a limestone lake and this makes for fabulous water quality. At times visibility is between ten and fifteen feet. Mind you, it hasn't always been as clear as this. The local Lough Ennell Trout Preservation Association has forced down pollution. Their focus has been on the feeder stream, where they've clamped down on the amount of agricultural waste, and sewage in particular, that has flowed into the lough.

It's got to be said immediately that Lough Ennell isn't an easy water. Even experts – and a lot of them come out of Dublin – agree that a brace can be considered a good day. Mind you, you've got to remember that many of the browns here are wild. Also, that brace of fish could easily be trout of between three and six pounds in weight. Yes, this is really very special fishing indeed.

The early season can be slow. Then there come huge hatches of Duck fly. Some days fish will feed so heavily that they absolutely gorge themselves. Your own artificial really is little more than a needle in a haystack, a blade of grass in that cow's field. Everything really takes off for the fly fisherman around the second week in May when the mayfly begin to appear. From mid May, therefore, to the end of the month, the fishing on Ennell is on full flow and this is when everyone wants to get afloat. The trout become catchable now, both during the day and in the evenings. Most locals would choose to go for a calm evening, just fishing a spent gnat as the light is beginning to go.

During the day, big dry flies work well – Wulffs, hackled mayflies and the local mosly may. Local lore has it that Pat Cleere ties the best flies for the loughs and his Green Peters really are something else.

After the mayfly come the sedge – Welshman's buttons – those small brown sedge with yellow underbodies. These pull up the big fish, especially in the late evening.

Towards the end of the season, throughout August and September, the lake fishes best on dark, windy days. Try big wet flies then, bumbles and daddies and so on. Look for the shallows around Belvedere House, a rambling mansion close to the shore. Goose Island and Rinn Point are also places to concentrate on.

Ennell is a comparatively safe lake to fish on – especially compared with those monsters in the west. You won't find too many rocks so it's pretty safe to go out on your own, especially in weather that isn't too wild. Go and enjoy.

SEASON – the brown trout season on Ennell runs from 1st March to 12th October.

TICKETS – Lough Ennell is free fishing, but *do* join the Lough Ennell Trout Preservation Association, which charges a very modest annual fee and you can rest assured that all your money goes towards the preservation of the water and the promotion of the wild brown trout stocks. It's simply not fair to travel to Ireland, reap the harvest of other people's work and not put anything back in. You can join at any number of outposts in the area.
You will need a boat to fish this water and the recommended contact here is Myles Hope, Lake View, Lynn, Mullingar, County Westmeath, Ireland.

DIRECTIONS – the lough cannot be missed to the south of Mullingar, on the right-hand side of the N8.

ACCOMMODATION – contact the Irish Tourist Board in Mullingar on 00353 (0)44 48650 for information about accommodation in the area.

AUGHRIM TROUT FISHERY – CO. WICKLOW

I think it's essential that I mention this extraordinary fishery, a little way south of Dublin. It's a four-acre lake set within a beautifully designed riverside park. The surroundings are quite gorgeous, but what makes it particularly important is the fact that the water is designed for disabled anglers. Of course, the non-disabled are more than welcome, encouraged even, in the hope that they will help their disabled fishing companions around the lake. Pathways are designed to make sure that wheelchairs can get close to the water and yet are in no danger of capsizing. There's a lovely pavilion, good facilities and an exotic verandah where you can have a drink, a sandwich and look out over the lake.

Glencar in County Kerry has many remote and open rivers, perfect for fly fishing.

The wild coastline of County Kerry.

One of Ireland's many hidden streams, awash with fish.

Rob Maloney, from Arrow Lodge in County Sligo, gets afloat after the pike.

Lough Cullin, as viewed from Healy's Hotel in County Mayo.

A perfect night for bass fishing.

Fly fishing on the River Mulcair in County Limerick.

It's an ideal spot for any family touring the Wicklow area – there's a whole host of things to do and see in this beautiful part of Ireland and the fishing here can be very good indeed. It's all about light line fishing really – go in the summer and you're unlikely to need anything more than a few buzzers and perhaps some Montanas. The fish fight well, are clearly visible and so can be stalked. But above all, it's this added element, knowing that disabled anglers are well catered for on a beautiful water, that really warms the heart. It's good to know that EU funds are from time to time put to really good use. The staff here are very helpful and positive. A tremendous day out.

SEASON – open all year.

TICKETS – contact Angling for All, Aughrim, County Wicklow on 00353 (0)402 36552. Prices are very reasonable – for example £5 for two hours fishing, two-fish limit, then catch and release; £9 for four hours fishing, two-fish limit, then catch and release; and £15 all day, three-fish limit, then catch and release.

DIRECTIONS – leave Dublin on the N11 following the coast through Bray and Wicklow as far as Arklow. Turn right onto the R747 to Aughrim. Go through the village, take a left at the traffic lights and the fishery is a short way down on the left. It is well-signposted.

ACCOMMODATION – contact Res Ireland on 0800 (0)66 866866 for information.

THE RIVER MULCAIR – CO. LIMERICK

The Mulcair is well-known to the Irish, but still something of a secret to those from abroad. It shouldn't be. On a good year the Mulcair produces well over three thousand salmon to rod and line, most of the grilse and summer salmon but with a few spring fish. There's also fantastic wild brown trout fishing to be had. But above all, it's the beauty of the river that fascinates. This is pastoral Ireland at its best and the Mulcair twists and turns through enchanting meadow and woodland. This is a place to lose yourself, confident of good fishing but seemingly light years away from the pressures of modern-day life. There's only one way to enjoy the Mulcair fully if you're not local and that's by checking into Millbank House and making use of the encyclopaedic knowledge of Richard Keays. Richard was born at Millbank and has been catching fish from the river there most of his life, so he is something of an authority with a charming and easy manner. Add all this to the grace of the building and his wife Sarah's sumptuous cooking, and you've got something pretty special.

The Mulcair rises in the mountains of County Tipperary and follows a south-easterly route where it enters the River Shannon two miles downstream of Castleconnell Fishery. Yes, *the* Castleconnell and, once again, Richard can both arrange tickets here and will prove the ablest of guides.

Although it's the Mulcair that wins my own particular heart, you'd be crazy not to fish Castleconnell for at least one day during your stay. All right, the Fishery isn't what it once was before the hydro scheme, but it's still a dashing, charismatic piece of water. Even if it doesn't produce the thirty and forty pounders of fifty years ago there are still magnificent fish to be had on what is an awesome piece of water.

⊡ SEASON – Open season March 1st – September 30th.

✎ TICKETS – A salmon licence is required and the Mulcair is an unlimited access fishery controlled by the Electricity Supply Board. Richard Keays can supply all the necessary ticketing.

⊨ → ACCOMMODATION AND DIRECTIONS – Millbank House is not easily found even though it's only eight miles from Limerick city. Deep in the heart of the sleepiest of countryside, it is two miles off the N24 Rosslair to Limerick road. Richard has good maps and I'd advise you to use them. Contact him on 00353 (0)61 36115 or by email at info@millbankhouse.com

BALLYVOLANE HOUSE – CO. CORK

I felt it essential to offer Ballyvolane to the angler visiting Ireland with his family. There are two lovely lakes in the grounds of this eighteenth-century mansion, both very well stocked, with rainbows going way above five pounds in weight. The two lakes are kept private, reserved for hotel residents, so you know you won't be fishing shoulder to shoulder.

There are quite a few such waters in Ireland, but there's something special about Ballyvolane. The accommodation is excellent and the beautifully-kept gardens have an aviary and a croquet lawn. There's also a little carp fishery planned, ideal for children.

Accommodation is excellent – it's been voted Ireland's best bed and breakfast by the AA – and the food is superb. Sandwiches can even be served down by the lakeside.

If you want to be a bit more ambitious, the hotel can arrange fishing on some six miles of the River Blackwater at a very reasonable cost. The house is situated in a wonderful area very close to Cork, in the valley of the River Bride – a tributary of the Blackwater – and a very interesting sea trout river at certain times. You can fly Stansted to Shannon now very cheaply, and this makes venues such as Ballyvolane more than accessible, even for a long weekend. A day on the lakes, an evening after sea trout on the Bride and a day on the Blackwater... a heavenly combination.

✎ TICKETS – contact Jeremy and Merrie Green, Ballyvolane House, Castlelyons, County Cork, on 00353 (0)25 36349.

→ DIRECTIONS – from Cork, take the N8 towards Fermoy, which will lead you to the River Bride. Just before the village of Rathcormack, turn right and follow the signs to the house.

LOUGH CURRANE – CO. KERRY

This is a magical place, about three miles long, perched down in the south-west of Ireland in County Kerry, next to the delightful town of Waterville. There can't

be a more beautiful place in Ireland: it's a magnificent area to take a holiday in. Dingle Bay is just to the north and Bantry Bay a little to the south. Fantastic cliffs, beautiful bathing and countryside to die for. But let's look at the fishing…

If you look back on the Irish specimen fish lists, you will see that Currane dominates when it comes to sea trout. For years, there have been huge, specimen sea trout running into the lough – a water that is free. You've only got to pay boat charges.

During the spring, most people troll for good-sized salmon and very large sea trout. Then, it's all a matter of tobies and rapalas. From May, you can start taking sea trout on the fly and it's brilliant sport. Fish wet flies lough-style – Bumbles, Green Peters, Daddies and so on. You will also pick up the occasional grilse in June and July.

You'll need a boat. These are for hire all around the shoreline, along with local ghillies. This is a very dangerous lake indeed, with many locks, and, being so close to the south-west coast, a storm can blow up at any time. This is a water where it's essential to take a ghilly – for the first day at least. You'd be mad not to. All the ghillies know exactly what they're talking about, but the famous family down here are the O'Sullivans. Like so much of what goes on in Ireland, you'll make contact with one of the clan in any of the local bars. One tip: evening fishing can be especially productive, so try to make sure that you can both be out until last knockings.

Currane is linked to the sea by a tiny river known locally as Butler's Fishery. This is available to those staying at the Butler Arms Hotel. It's private fishing for hotel guests but can be tremendously good, especially when grilse are running. And, finally, if the water is really high, consider Lough Capal, a very small water situated just above Lough Currane itself and linked by streams. When the water is high, the very biggest sea trout run up into this tiny lough. Thrilling stuff.

SEASON – mid-January to mid-September (salmon); March to September (sea trout).
TICKETS – free fishing, but you will need a boat. These are widely available.
DIRECTIONS – Currane is just south-west of Waterville, easily seen from the N70 road.
ACCOMMODATION – Recommended is the Butler Arms at Waterville on 00353 (0)66 9474144, or you can contact the Tourist Information office at Waterville, on 00353 (0)66 9474646, which is open from May to mid-September.

GLENCAR HOUSE AND FISHERY – CO. KERRY

Glencar was another fishery unknown to me until 2002 when I fell in love with the charming hotel, the landscape and the fabulous diversity of the fishing. The Upper Caragh River is a glorious, tumbling spate river that has seven named beats, all with fishing huts, all offering excellent fly fishing opportunities. The river is still recognised as a spring salmon river but grilse enter in number throughout May and June, with summer salmon following along later. This means that there are generally fish in the river that are fresh and catchable.

Glencar also offers access to three loughs, Caragh, Cloon and Acoose. Cloon is a particular favourite of mine: so wild, so remote and starkly beautiful. Salmon run the lough but there's also really good trout fishing to be enjoyed. But in a place so beautiful, it's impossible not to have one of the days of your life.

If all this doesn't tempt you there are even three smaller tributaries of the main river itself: the Brida, the Owenroe and the Little Caragh. Again, at the right times of year, these are inundated with salmon and there are always plenty of brown trout, too.

There's a relaxed feel to Glencar and the fishery. It's a real fisherman's haunt and the bar talk is almost exclusively of flies, beats and conditions. You're soon made to feel such a part of the place that, believe me, it's an absolute wrench to leave.

SEASON – Salmon fishing runs from 1st February to 30th September. Brown trout fishing opens on 15th March and ends on 12th October.
Tickets: – A state licence is needed for salmon. Daily rates vary according to the time of year.
ACCOMMODATION – Glencar House has eighteen rooms. Telephone 00353 (0)66 9760102. Email info@glencarhouse.com
DIRECTIONS – Like all good fishing hotels, Glencar is absolutely lost in the wilds of remotest Kerry. You will find Killorglin on the N70. Glencar is to the south: ask for directions in the town. From about five miles, an elaborate system of signposts guides you in!

IRELAND'S COASTLINE

This is really something for the adventurous angler, perhaps the man on holiday looking for something a bit different. You've got to realise that Ireland has an extraordinary number of bays, estuaries, inflowing streams, lagoons... you name it, everything is there for incoming shoals of sea trout, bass and mullet. Of course, I'm not saying that every estuary and river mouth has superb sea trout fishing, but a little exploration can throw up some amazing results.

Obviously, you've got to check that fishing is available, but normally you can get all the details you want by asking at the nearest bar. The sea trout run best in most parts of Ireland through June, July and August. Try to get out on a rising tide, especially if it coincides with the late evening or dusk. Flies? Well, up in Donegal and Sligo, locals fish Rogan's Gadget as, with its silver belly and olive back, it certainly looks like a sand eel, the basis of the sea trout diet close inshore. Don't fish the flies slowly. Get them going near the surface with a bit of action. Often you'll see a bigger 'v' following your own fly in. Try casting into the current and letting the flow speed the flies' retrieve further. But do experiment. You'll find that a different retrieve pattern is needed from one night to the next, even from one hour to the next at times.

Keep on the move until you contact, or at least see, fish. If you see locals congregate, you can be pretty sure that they know a hotspot. You'll get good, honest advice and a warm welcome. They like to see visitors doing something a little out of the ordinary.

It's with real trepidation that I recommend fly fishing for mullet! These can be infuriatingly difficult to catch, but there are so many of them in shallow Irish waters throughout the summer that they can provide a really thrilling alternative to trout and salmon. Again, this is very wild fishing and you need to ask the locals for a bit of advice. Ideally, you're looking for lagoons where you can wade with security, in water that's no more than a couple of feet deep. You'll find that the mullet follow very skinny water indeed, coming in at the beginning of the flow. Often you'll see them working, tails out of the water, muddying the bottom. Wade very carefully until you get to within casting distance and put down as light a line as you can. Obviously, a floating line is all you'll need with any small, dark patterns – any spider imitation should be a good kick-off. Try them on a size fourteen hook initially, but go up or down if you're not getting any response. A slow, careful retrieve generally works better, and be prepared for quite a sharp, snaggy take. And then fireworks!

Do, always, make sure that you are investigating safe areas. Check up with locals about tides and any potential dangers. Never take risks and always make sure that you stay absolutely within reach of land.

This is truly wild fishing and it's wild fishing that Ireland is in essence about. There's no point talking about logistics here. Most of the fishing will be free and most of the fishing is at its best from May through to September. Nor is there any point talking about directions. If you're anywhere near the coast then the chances are that there will be areas to investigate. Good luck, and happy exploring.

❧ HIGHLY RECOMMENDED FISHERIES ❧

- *The Blackwater, County Waterford. Contact the Blackwater Lodge fishery on 00353 (0)58 60235. Recommended accommodation and first-rate fishing. One of the joys of Blackwater Lodge is its wide variety of beats that cater for fly, spinner and bait fishing. Furthermore, as the beats are so widely spread up and down the river, there is always a prime chance of contacting fish.*
- *Rathbeggan Lakes, Dublin. Phone 00353 (0)1 8240197 for details. Very close to the centre of Dublin. A new water offering very good fishing and many facilities, including secure parking. A brave venture.*
- *Springwater Fly Fishery, County Antrim, Northern Ireland. A very promising water. A lot of fish caught on lures.*
- *The Caragh Fishery, County Kerry. Call on 00353 (0)66 9760102. Offers superb river salmon fishing and excellent lough browns.*
- *Lough Sheelin, County Westmeath. One of Ireland's truly great brown trout fishery. Contact Cullens' Fishing Lodge on 00353 (0)43 81311.*

WHERE TO
COARSE FSH
IN IRELAND

COARSE-FISHING SITES
IN IRELAND

1. Lough Mask
2. Lough Corrib
3. Loughs Conn & Cullin
4. Lough Arrow
5. Lough Key
6. Carrick-on-Shannon
7. Lough Ree
8. Athlone
9. Lough Derg
10. River Bann
11. Lower Lough Erne
12. Grand Canal
13. Lough Muckno

14. Upper River Bann
15. The River Erne
16. The River Blackwater
17. Lough Allen
18. Royal Canal
19. Lough Muck
20. Clay Lake

'The more I catch, the more I realise I know next to nothing about pike fishing in this country. Each season I learn more about old waters and find so many new ones that you hardly know where to cast next. Only the other day I heard about a lough – a small one, virtually unfished – and it produced a thirty-four-pounder to the first guys to go there. Just like that. I could tell you similar stories for a week on end.'

DAVID OVERY, IRISH WRITER AND PIKE LEGEND

David Overy is one of Ireland's best known and certainly most successful pike anglers, and I well remember this conversation with him over breakfast in one of Dublin's finest hotels.

It is no wonder that Ireland has drawn pike fishermen to its waters for well over a hundred years now. The great trout-rich loughs and bream-infested rivers have produced some of the world's biggest pike – and if you only half believe the legends, there are pike to put shark to shame! Of course, Ireland is a bit like that: it's a land of mists and magic, and there are times when you are afloat on a water like Mask or Corrib when you can believe that just about anything is underneath you. Mind you, you would probably be right!

Even if pike are not your thing, Ireland is still bound to have a huge amount to offer the coarse fisherman. The bream fishing is probably the best in the world. There are rudd to die for. Where else can you catch endless amounts of five- and six-pound tench from scores of waters that are all but virgin?

Coarse Fishing

LOUGHS CONN, CULLIN AND THE SURROUNDING RIVERS – CO. MAYO

I don't want to make a huge deal about this because my experience of the coarse fishing in this area is quite limited. However, in two short days I did begin to appreciate its extraordinary potential. As it is a top fly fishing venue, it was with fly fishing in mind that I made my way to the area in September 2002. There were plenty of salmon in Conn but they were difficult to tempt. The trout were very dour. Enjoying all types of fishing, I looked for alternatives.

I was told that the pike fishing is excellent, but that didn't really excite me. I was also told about the rudd of Cullin, and although I failed to catch I saw some great-looking specimens and some large shoals of admittedly fidgety fish. I was actually trying for them with fly gear and I'm sure that if I'd had bread or maggots it would have been quite a different matter. I also heard that several of the rivers that enter into Lough Conn, notably up the western shore, have amazing roach fishing possibilities.

Accordingly, I explored. I found one particular stream which I think is all but nameless, and close to the road bridge there were one or two areas where people had obviously fished. I asked for permission at a nearby cottage and the man stared at me as though I was quite mad. Fish away I was told, nobody cares about the roach.

An hour later on float-fished bread I landed a roach of about one and a half pounds. Two hours later, I had another couple slightly bigger. An ex-pat English angler wandered along and told me the whole story. It seems that he fishes from time to time – hence the flattened down areas – and generally catches roach to two and a half pounds! Considering he puts in a couple of hours or so a week that's not bad, and I think it's safe to say that the potential is pretty well untapped. This is a wild, lovely, lonely region and if you're prepared to ask locals, perhaps treating them to a pint of Guinness, the potential could be extraordinary for any angler with a pioneering bent.

But isn't that what coarse fishing in Ireland is all about? Of course, you can go to the well-trodden, well-signposted areas, but most places in Ireland you can find coarse fishing that's virtually unknown. There are some real gems waiting to be discovered.

SEASON – Year round.

TICKETS – No state licence needed, but do ask for the landowner's permission to fish.

ACCOMMODATION AND DIRECTIONS – Healy's Hotel on the R310 at Pontoon is primarily a fly fishing hotel, but it's very relaxed and a great spot for any angler. English guide Graham Williams has a thorough knowledge of the area, which he will happily share. Telephone 00353 (0)94 56443. Email info@healyspontoon.com

LOUGH ARROW PIKING – CO. SLIGO

I say Lough Arrow only because this beautiful water does have pike and it is the geographical heart of the area to be discussed. It was with Rob Maloney, proprietor of that excellent trout fisherman's lodging Arrow Lodge, that I was alerted to the huge possibilities of pike fishing the area. Rob adopts two slightly unusual approaches. Firstly, he invariably fly fishes for pike and whilst this might mean he doesn't catch the very biggest in any water it certainly doesn't hold him back in numbers landed. He uses stout tackle – generally nine or ten weight – and a selection of streamer type flies.

Secondly, he uses a u-boat – a portable float tube, that is – to manoeuvre himself into the tightest, most inaccessible corners. This allows huge flexibility; it's a real step forward that more coarse fishers ought to take.

However, naturally, you don't have to either fly fish or get yourself afloat to enjoy the piking that Rob can show you. He reckons that within minutes of motoring time from the lodge he could take you to any one of twenty or thirty all but unfished trout loughs. This is really something: I visited four with Rob over a couple of days and was stunned. Every water was remote, beautiful and mostly unfished. The pike stocks were rampant, and although we caught nothing above upper teens in weight, there's no doubt that fish well into the upper twenties and thirties certainly exist.

I do advise you to contact Rob: this is a wonderful part of the world with a colossal amount of piking, straight out of Irish fishing legend. You can really feel like a piking pioneer around here, and goodness knows what a big dead bait would have turned up if presented properly on any one of Rob's magnificent, tucked-away paradises.

SEASON – Pike fishing goes well through most of the winter, but really begins to pick up again in February and March. The summer months can be very productive also.

TICKETS – There is no statutory rod licence for coarse fishing, but it's important to ask the landowner for permission to cross the land and fish the water. This is generally given. Rob Maloney knows the landowners in question and he's welcomed with a cheery smile.

ACCOMMODATION – Contact Rob at Arrow Lodge on 00353 (0)79 66298 or email him at rob@arrowlodge.com

DIRECTIONS – Lough Arrow is in the northwest of Southern Ireland, north of Boyle. Approach it on the N4 from the town. Rob will give instructions to the Lodge from there. He also has float tubes that he can lend you, but I'd advise some supervision from him first!

THE SHANNON

The Shannon is a magnificent, extraordinary watercourse: a hundred and sixty miles long with a catchment area taking in the greater part of central Ireland. It's a limestone river, rich in weed and food, gently flowing for the most part, but with deep glides and, fascinatingly, an amazing number of loughs and lagoons off its spinal cord. To know the Shannon in a dozen life-times would be all but impossible. There's just so much water to fish, so much of it hidden and secretive: only accessible, naturally enough, by boat. The Irish themselves adore the Shannon. It's a magnet to them; hardly surprising given the huge number of specimen fish that it's produced over the decades. Pike, bream, rudd, perch – you name it, the Shannon holds it. So, in many ways, the Shannon is the core of coarse fishing throughout Ireland but, with my few attempts on the river, how could I possibly begin to describe it? I couldn't. Enter my dear friend from Dublin, Charlie Stuart – a man who's lived his leisure life on the great river.

'Let's take the northern area first, from Lough Key down to Carrick-on-Shannon. You could spend the best part of a year exploring this area, if not your entire life. The list of species to be caught is breathtaking, from the humble roach to regular catches of

❧ NIGHT-FISHING BASICS ❧

Night fishing can sometimes give you the edge, especially during hot weather. However, it is a specialised technique, and following a few basic guidelines can help to make your expedition successful and safe.
- *Don't go on your own for your first few sessions; go along with a friend. It's even better if he or she has night-fishing experience.*
- *Don't night fish in water that you don't have any experience of. Always visit the swim that you intend to visit at night during the daytime, so you can get the feel of it and note down any over-hanging trees or other possible problems after dark.*
- *Lay everything around you that you might need during the darkness whilst it is still light. Make sure there is an order to all this so you know exactly where you can lay your hands on things in the blackness.*
- *Always have one big torch for emergencies.*
- *Always take a small torch for the little fiddly jobs such as rebaiting.*
- *A headlamp like miners used to use is a good idea, especially when you're playing fish and you need both hands free.*
- *Always take plenty of warm clothes, even if the day has been hot. Temperatures can plummet after dark.*
- *Take plenty of food and warm drinks. No alcohol!*
- *If you do a lot of night fishing, it is a good idea to make sure your torch is mid-red rather than white light. This can be done by using a red bulb or by colouring the torch face with a red marker pen. Red light is less likely to scare fish and is kinder on the eyes.*
- *Things that go bump in the night. Remember that the strange wheezing that is coming from that nearby bush is more likely to be a hedgehog than a werewolf! The world can seem weird after dark, but there is always a rational explanation for everything.*

big double-figure pike. At **Lough Key** you can gain access to the water by driving from Carrick towards Boyle in County Roscommon. About four miles outside Carrick, you will come across Lough Key Forest Park, which itself is a beautiful spot to visit. If you enter the park you will see a large tower, below which are jetties. It's from these that I've had some of my best bream and perch fishing ever. Lough Key produced an Irish record pike tipping the scales at thirty-nine pounds and three ounces, so it's well worth a visit for big predators. The lake is easily accessible for pleasure craft, so you won't have any shortage of company. What I'm saying is that even though I've had bags of bream well over a hundred pounds, being a night owl helps. You'll find they tend to feed after midnight until four or five o'clock in the morning (later on a dull day).

'Moving downstream, we'll come to the smaller water of **Oakport Lough** behind the village of Knockvicar. It's a lake that's an absolute must for any keen piker. Boat hire is available in the village and the northern shore of this reed-lined water seems to produce the best fishing. The best methods by far are trolled or wobbled dead baits. As the lake is virtually inaccessible overland, you've got to organise boat hire. Just ask at the bar and you'll be sent in the right direction.

A little further down the Shannon you will come across **Lough Drumharlow**. This is an ideal water for the general all-rounder and the family on holiday. It produces bags of roach, tench and bream and, as you'd expect, significant numbers of good double-figure pike. The lake is accessible from the road but some anglers opt for the tranquillity of fishing from the island. Boat hire is essential to get you over and, once again, simply ask at that bar! I always say that the coarse fishing in Ireland is free but you've got to have a pound or two in your pocket for the odd Guinness!

'Having covered the local lakes of the northern section, I should add that there are sections of river here that are well worth a visit. Large areas of the banks are unfishable, but if you can get on the water, you will be surprised at the amazing clarity of the water, and you can actually see shoals of fish cruising along the riverbed. It's really brilliant to watch the bream and tench, moving slowly, tipping to feed, kicking up clouds of silt. It gets the heart beating, I can tell you. I should mention the area around Carrick-on-Shannon itself here. There are impressive bags of fish put together here, even in the harbour of the town centre, but the quality of the water does leave a lot to be desired and you won't get that clarity I was just talking about. Having said that, the town itself is well worth a visit after a session, because the hospitality and nightlife would rejuvenate the bones of the wettest fisherman!

'Moving down south from Carrick you enter a maze of waters that you could lose yourself in. The river splits in two directions, with the main section flowing through the settlement of Jamestown, while the other section is cut off through the Albert canal. The canal itself is not really worth a visit before reaching Albert Lough, due to the volume of boat traffic that passes along its length. Below Albert Lough, the canal rejoins the river to flow into **Lough Boderg**, which in turn flows into **Lough Bofinn**. It is at the meeting of these two waters that the river narrows. This is probably the best location on the two waters, as the shoreline is protected by a large forest, which gives you good shelter and comfortable fishing. The sport in this area is generally excellent, but be prepared to carry large amounts of ground bait – a good sharper would not go amiss! Bags include bream up to six pound plus and some pristine tench. Just north of Roosky is the beautiful village of **Dromod**. I've spent many a pleasant evening fishing in the harbour here, but again you have to be prepared to burn the midnight oil, as it's very busy during the day. The fish move back at dusk and from about midnight onwards, as things quieten down, large shoals of bream begin to reclaim the harbour as their own. Bags of over a hundred pounds are not uncommon and, with the added benefit of public lighting, you can fish and see what you're doing until the early hours.

'If we move on again south towards **Rooskey**, again we'll find a busy village for the boating fraternity. However, I would really recommend a visit to the lough here, as there is a lovely quiet backwater behind the lough keeper's cottage. I've caught some great perch here, many weighing over two pounds. If you prefer quantity, then the shoals of roach and perch will keep you occupied for hours – a great place for kids too.

'Let's have a look at the middle Shannon now, the famous area around Athlone and Lough Ree. Many people have thought about writing a book on **Lough Ree** itself alone, but here's just a short introduction. On the northern end of the lake sits the town of Lanesborough – a place that in recent years has become a honey-pot for visiting anglers. The main attraction is the location of the local power station with its outflow of warm water. To say that you have to be up early to have access to a swim would be an understatement – this is what we all know as a really serious hotspot! It seems that the fish are attracted to the warmer climate that the outflow brings and the anglers follow. Bags of even a hundred and fifty pounds plus are not unusual. You'll find roach, bream, roach/bream hybrids, tench, rudd and any amount of perch. It's well worth a visit but, as I've said, you've got to arrive early or you'll be disappointed.

'Moving south on the lake down the eastern shoreline, you come across **Inny Bay**, where the River Inny itself enters the lake. This is a spot that has become renowned for massive shoals of bream. Indeed, one of my pals once said that he had to stop spinning for pike as he was foul-hooking so many bream. It's a must for the visiting angler if you have the nerve to put a really big bag together. On the opposite side of the lake you have **Hodson Bay**, another Mecca for big bream bags. There's a hotel just above the area and you can see people landing fish from the bar itself.

'Now we're at **Shannonbridge**, about to move down to Lough Derg itself. Shannonbridge is a little village on the border of County Galway and even without the brilliant fishing it would be worth a visit for its history. Its main street crosses the river over an impressive nineteen-arch bridge – hence the name. Beside the bridge is a massive fortress built by the British during the Napoleonic Wars back in the early 19th century. From this building, you will be able to see most of the area that you'll want to fish. I personally have had many wonderful evenings fishing in Shannonbridge, but make a decision about what method you are going to use before you start.

'This is important, as different species abound in the area and the current tends to be a little faster on this stretch of the river. Trotting is a winner, but so is ledgering. I've had good bags of tench and bream, and endless amounts of roach and rudd. A little downstream of the town you'll find a cutting used by boats navigating the river, and I've had some of my best pike fishing in the area at the entrance of this. Try a wobbled roach, drifting in and out of the current, and expect fish well into double figures.

'Now we're at Shannon harbour, which lies on the Grand Canal, just before its entrance to the river. Running alongside the canal is the **River Brosna**. I've had some really impressive fishing on this river just where it joins the main Shannon. In one session, for example, I caught nine pike to fourteen pounds, all falling to a float-fished dead rudd. I must hasten to remind you that live baiting on these waters is illegal. Moving downstream to the town of Banagher, you'll find a large harbour there and the river tends to pick up momentum. In fact, you've got really quite a strong current through the whole stretch. The banks around the town tend to be very difficult to fish because they're marshy, known locally as the Callows. However, below the town of Banagher you will come upon a large weir and lough known as **Meelick**. It's here that the fishing tends to become more comfortable and you'll find some well-prepared swims on the western side of the river. If you read Fred Buller's Domesday Book of Pike you'll see that a fish of some sixty-nine inches in length was found dead here. The estimated weight was ninety pounds. I will leave that to your imagination and your scepticism, but remember that if you were to land a fish of half that weight you would hold the Irish record! It would beat the river record by over three pounds.

'The town of **Portumna** lies on the northern shores of Lough Derg; this stretch of water has produced some massive fish and excellent sport for visitors and locals alike. The river in the area of Portumna is very deep and in winter this acts as a magnet to the pike. Let's move now into **Lough Derg**, which is awe-inspiring! There's so much water that you could spend a lifetime exploring. The massive lough is riddled with bays and islands, and my advice is to search out secluded bays, bait up and wait for the bream to come in. Alternatively, pole quietly around in a small boat looking for the rudd shoals. I needn't say a word to you about the pike fishing. Just take one quick look at the Domesday Book: you'll see that there are thirteen entries for Lough Derg alone.

'Leaving Lough Derg, you'll come to the villages of **Killaloe** and **O'Brien's Bridge**, both popular venues for the coarse angler. You'll find many visitors there.

'I've spent so many weeks cruising the Shannon, and yet every time I visit I discover a new venue and it's like starting afresh. In fact, I don't think there's anybody that could know the whole Shannon system. You could spend a lifetime on it and still not scratch the surface. Mind you, that doesn't mean to say that you have to be an expert to catch fish. You don't. You won't find better coarse fishing anywhere in Europe.'

CONTACT – for angling information for the Shannon region contact Shannon Development, Shannon Town Centre, County Clare, on 00353 (0)61 361555. Garry Kenny,

Palmerstown Stores, Portumna, on 00353 (0)509 41071, will advise on fishing in the northern Lough Derg area. At Shannonbridge, contact Dermot Killeen, Bar and Grocery, Main Street, on 00353 (0)905 74112. In Roosky, contact Key Enterprises and Lakeland Bait.
▭ ACCOMMODATION – for information, contact Limerick Tourist Board on 00353 (0)61 317522, or Athlone Tourist Board on 00353 (0)902 94630.

BREAM FISHING – RIVER BANN AND LOUGH ERNE, NORTHERN IRELAND

The bream fishing in Ireland is arguably the best that you'll find anywhere in the world. There are huge shoals of fish in an endless number of areas. Moreover, these are fish that are rarely pursued – you'll generally find the Irish only interested in things with an adipose fin on them!

However, even though this is breaming paradise, the fish don't give themselves up easily and you've got to work quite hard if you want to reap the ultimate harvest.

There are several rules. In the summer, you've got to think about fishing early and late, if not through the night. If the water is clear and the sun is bright, don't expect to catch a good number of fish. Then you've go to ground bait heavily. These are very big shoals and they're hungry fish. If you just put out half a pint of maggots you'll hold a shoal of bream for half a minute. The best plan is to work out an ambush area, feed heavily in the late afternoon and wait for the bream to move over it in the evening. The majority of bream in Ireland are uneducated when it comes to tackle but they do want a lot of food to go down over.

Bear in mind the weather conditions. Ireland can change dramatically from one moment to the next. If the winds are warm and wet from the southwest and the temperatures are mild, then you can expect to find bream in shallow water. If, however, there's a dip in water temperature, look for them in water of over ten feet deep.

When it comes to what you give the bream, think things out carefully. It's no good just ground baiting with a couple of pounds – you've really got to pile it in and, above all, you've got to mix things into the ground bait that will keep the fish interested. Casters are obviously good, but a gallon or so, which is what you'd need, does cost a fair amount. So also with chopped worms – a few pounds of those wouldn't go amiss either. Instead, try a dozen cans of sweetcorn, stewed wheat, pellets and so on. What you've got to do is to keep a shoal of bream, anything up to five hundred fish strong, interested for hours on end.

Remember that the bream are not tackle shy and you'll find that they fight much harder in Ireland than they do in England. This means that you can go comparatively heavy – think about a size twelve hook and main line of four or five pounds straight through. There's also the point that a big tench could come along at any moment as well.

All the usual techniques do well but probably most big bags are built up with a swim feeder. It makes sense to cast your feeder to the perimeter of activity. If you put it right in the centre of the shoal, not only do you run the risk of disturbing the fish, especially in shallow water, but you've also got to get the hooked bream out. Fishing the edges, you might not get a bite instantly, but you won't break the shoal up.

If you don't fancy the idea of fishing through the night on holiday, try ground baiting at nine or ten o'clock in the evening. Put out a great number of small balls of bait and then return at first light – so not too much Guinness! With any luck, the bream will have moved in over the ground bait overnight and still be there – giving you three or four hours' hectic sport before packing up for breakfast and a day trip!

In Northern Ireland, **Portglenone** on the lower River Bann in Antrim has become a top venue. You'll find eighty purpose-made fishing stands there, all with good access.
CONTACT – Smith's Tackle in Ballymoney, on 028 2766 4259.

Try also **Lower Lough Erne** at Trory, Fermanagh. This is excellent in the springtime when the water starts to warm up. There are several purpose-built concrete fishing stands, and you can catch fish here nicely on the waggler.
CONTACT – Field and Stream in Enniskillen, on 028 6632 2114.

In the south, try **Ballycullian Lake**, Corrofin, Galway. A brilliant lake with big bays – a major venue for big bream. Fish to ten pounds. The Shannon Regional Fisheries Board has provided boat stands in several areas. Excellent.
CONTACT – Michael Cleary, Shannon Regional Fisheries Board, on 00353 (0)65 6837675.

The **Grand Canal**, Edenderry, Offaly. The Grand Canal flows close to this town situated thirty miles west of Dublin. It is a coloured water with masses of bream and some carp.
CONTACT – Padraic Kelly on 00353 (0)405 32071.

Lough Muckno, Castleblayney, Monaghan. This is a large lake with big bream stocks. Pre-baiting very important here.
CONTACT – Jim Mc Mahon on 00353 (0)42 9661714.

Remember that bream are very well spread throughout the entire island, both north and south. There are huge numbers of rivers, loughs and pools with bream fishing freely available. Remember the old advice: go into the bar and order a Guinness!

ROACH ON THE BLACKWATER, THE BANN AND THE ERNE

The roach fishing in Ireland has become a phenomenon. They've probably been present in the country for about a hundred and twenty years, and have spread rapidly – partly through natural causes and sometimes because of anglers

transporting them for live baits (but not now that live baiting in the south is illegal). Roach have undoubtedly become an important part of the Irish angling touring scene and some of my own first trips to Ireland were superb for the brilliant roach fishing down in the Munster Blackwater. What fishing it was back in the 1970s – the great roach explosion in the Blackwater around the Moy and Cappoquin. In fact, the renowned bacon factory at Cappoquin was the centre of it all. Dreadful times! By that I mean the river there fished best when the pigs were brought in to be slaughtered. A pipe ran into the river with gallons of congealed blood washing away in the stream. The roach, sea trout and seagulls went barmy! I confess, to my horror these days, I joined in the glut and had many a roach to just about two pounds and some big, big dace.

On the Blackwater, you didn't have to fish in such appalling surroundings to catch big roach. They were, and are still, freely available. In fact, today, the roach have spread so widely it's not difficult to find them anywhere. Only last year I enjoyed some fantastic roach fishing in Northern Ireland, around **Enniskillen** on Upper Lough Erne. The roach just seemed to come and to come. Fish all the way up to a pound on float-fished maggots just tripping bottom. Tremendous fishing.

Remember that, by and large, the roach in Ireland are less tackle shy than those in England. You can't always get away with heavier tackle and certainly not crude bait presentation, but you can afford to scale up a little bit. Feeding, too, must be done more heavily. In England we're used to scattering a pinch of maggots every now and again: over in Ireland you've got to be bolder if you're going to hold a shoal.

Try the **Upper River Bann**, Portadown, Armagh. Portadown used to be the hotspot for huge roach catches and is now recovering well after a bit of a slump. Big bags of roach are still possible, and you can catch fish nudging the two pound mark.
CONTACT – Premier Angling, Lurgan, on 028 3832 5204.

The **River Erne**, Enniskillen, Fermanagh, once rewrote the record books, and even today there is some magnificent fishing available in the area. It's a tremendous centre for all manner of species, but the roach fishing must be amongst the best in Europe. Plenty of fish, and some very big ones indeed. Local knowledge is important.
CONTACT – Field and Stream, Enniskillen, on 028 6632 2114.

Down in the south, the **River Blackwater** at **Fermoy** in County Cork is unbeatable. This is a big river, running through the town, full of roach and dace. Look for swims around the main town bridge and the renowned hospital stretch. There's great trotting, providing you work at the swim with plenty of feed. Everybody is willing to give you advice here. It's a magnet for anglers, and championship matches are held. You might not catch the really big roach of yesteryear, but there'll be some cracking specimens.
CONTACT – Pat Barrie on 00353 (0)25 36187.

Don't be afraid to explore the entire Blackwater – Cappoquin still produces some brilliant roach. There are all sorts of access points along the river, a most attractive water and a roach fisherman's paradise.

PIKE ON THE LOUGHS AND THE RIVER SUCK

Pike fishing in Ireland is still remarkable, though there have been problems in the recent past. At one stage, a great number of anglers from continental Europe were visiting Ireland, catching sizeable pike and killing them to take home the heads as trophies. Fortunately, this practice has just about ceased. Pike have also been remorselessly culled in some of the premier trout waters. This is still going on to some degree, but increasingly there is an acceptance that big pike actually do a water good and it's the jacks that have to be removed.

Having said all that, Ireland remains a pike angler's dream. Pike have been resident here for about four hundred years; they immediately found Irish waters to their liking. Pike thrive on neglect, and for many decades were certainly neglected! When the Victorians began to fish for them in the late 19th century they found pike fishing beyond their wildest dreams. The pike grow particularly quickly in the limestone loughs – rich feed for trout and coarse fish means good growing conditions for the pike. Not only is there plenty of day-to-day food for pike in most Irish waters, but there are also added bonuses. Some of the huge pike in the past have definitely benefited from runs of salmon, sea trout, eels and even shad. In short, Ireland has everything that big pike need: large, rich, under-pressured waters, full of nutritious prey fish.

Catching very big pike from Ireland is not always easy. On some of the large waters such as Mask, Corrib, Derg, Ree and Neagh, location is always a problem. You can either go on local knowledge or take an echo sounder with you. You'll often be able to locate shoals of prey fish by bream and roach, and you'll certainly be able to discover drop-offs, plateaux and any other obvious fish holding areas. On watercourses such as Lough Erne, location is easier – the pike tend to follow the big shoals of bream and roach, so a good starting place is where you find pleasure anglers doing very well.

To fish Ireland successfully for pike you have to have mobility, and that almost always means a boat. Fortunately, every single village in Ireland next to a waterway is well geared up for this. What I have found, however, is that it sometimes pays to take your own engine across. Irish engines are not always as reliable as they should be!

You've got to remember that live baiting is banned in the south but that doesn't mean that your chances are restricted at all. Dead baiting works very well and most of the waters are clear enough to provide excellent lure fishing.

I recently enjoyed wonderful pike fishing over a three-day period on **Upper Lough Erne**, just south of Enniskillen. My very first cast with a gold Super Shad resulted in a twenty-five pound pike! Things don't get better than that. For the rest of the stay I continued to do well with big, flashy plugs. It was largely a case of moving slowly

43

around the waterways, exploring with a plug and, when fish were found, anchoring up and putting out a couple of dead baits. The fish averaged a very high size – around twelve to fourteen pounds – and another couple of twenties came to the net. All the fish were in superb condition, and even though it was at the peak of the fishing season, we only saw two other pike anglers out over the weekend. That is piking in Ireland for you: you can find yourself on a magnificent water and be virtually alone.

My other major experiences of pike in Ireland have been on **Loughs Corrib and Mask** and the potential here is awesome. Netting has reduced numbers to some degree, but my own belief is that this has only pushed up the possible potential size. I don't think anybody who fishes these waters is in any doubt that forties and even fifties possibly exist. Mind you, fishing can be heart-breaking. Because there aren't many pike in the waters, it's difficult to build up a picture of their movements. You're very much alone. The best bet, in my opinion, is to explore as much water as possible with big spinners and plugs. Once again, when you've found fish, it pays to anchor up and investigate more thoroughly with dead baits. In very heavy weather it's possible to moor up behind the islands on the big loughs, put out a couple of dead baits and wait. This can be slow fishing, but when the float cocks and the line begins to pull out, your heart really is in your mouth. This could certainly be the fish of your dreams.

It is very difficult to give precise locations for pike fishing. It is so widely available and people will help you in every way they can. For anybody taking their car over to Ireland, it could well be that you'll be landing in Dublin. If so, then Dave McBride is the perfect man to inspire you and set you on your way. He's a fund of information when it comes to all manner of pike fishing and general coarse fishing in Ireland.

✎ CONTACT – Dave McBride, Clanbrassil Street, Dublin 2, on 00353 (0)1 4530266.

One hot area is the River Suck around **Castlecoote** and **Athleague**, Roscommon. There are big bags of bream roach and hybrids, and these seem to attract large pike. In recent years there have been rumours of big thirties being caught – well worth checking out.

✎ CONTACT – Mrs Holmes on 00353 (0)43 21491.

In the west, there is excellent fishing on **Loughs Corrib, Mask, Coolin and Nafooey**.

✎ CONTACT – John O'Donnell on 00353 (0)92 46157 for information on boats in the area.

⊢ ACCOMMODATION – Fairhill Guesthouse, Clonbur, on 00353 (0)92 46176, accommodates anglers and arranges fishing trips with boatmen.

Cong is a fascinating area and offers excellent pike fishing.

✎ CONTACT – Michael Ryan, River Lodge, Cong, on 00353 (0)92 46057, regarding boats. O'Connor's Tackle Shop in Cong also offers up-to-the-minute information.

Ballinrobe and **Tourmakready** are excellent centres on Lough Mask.

✎ CONTACT – Dermot O'Connor's Tackle Shop on Main Street, Ballinrobe. There are

centres for boat hire at Cushlough Pier, Rosshill Park and Cahir Pier.
Contact also Derry Park Lodge Angling Centre, on 00353 (0)92 44081, at Tourmakready.

The **Erne system** offers extremely good piking.
  ✏ CONTACT – Field and Stream, Enniskillen, on 028 6632 2114, offers excellent advice.
  ⊨ ACCOMMODATION – Rossahilly House, on 028 6632 2352, is a wonderful guesthouse, right on the water and offering brilliant bream and pike fishing. Advice is freely given. There is also marvellous accommodation on Bell Isle, just south of Enniskillen on Upper Lough Erne, and boats are available. Call Bell Isle Estate, Lisbellaw, Enniskillen, County Fermanagh, on 028 6638 7231.

In Ireland it is so easy to get off the beaten track and try a totally new water. How about **Lough Arrow** in County Sligo? This is revered first and foremost as a big trout water, but there are also some excellent pike.
  ✏ CONTACT – Stephanie and Robert Maloney at Arrow Lodge, Kilmactranny, Via Boyle, for details, on 00353 (0)79 66298.

⊱ CLEARWATER RUDD ⊰

Ireland has many sparkling coarse fishing alternatives on offer but perhaps the most dramatic is the rudd fishing on the crystal-clear limestone loughs. Fishing for them, however, can be a frustrating business.
- *Take your time as you move around the water – you'll almost certainly need a boat and either oars or an electric engine will be necessary.*
- *Drift more than you row.*
- *Scan the water with binoculars, looking for any surface activity.*
- *Choose warm, bright, comparatively still days.*
- *Look for reedy bays, water lilies – anything that gives the flitting rudd shoals some sense of security.*
- *Drift pieces of floating bread downstream and watch through binoculars to see rising fish at a distance.*
- *If fish are located, use a three- or four-pound line, a size eight hook and either a big piece of flake or a piece of floating crust about the size of a fifty pence piece.*
- *Dunk both the flake or the crust to give added weight for casting distance.*
- *Either attach a small float or watch the line for a take.*
- *When a rudd is hooked, hustle it away from the rest of the shoal as quickly as possible. Release all fish caught immediately. Rudd are arguably the most beautiful fish in the British Isles and keep nets do absolutely nothing for their appearance.*

TENCH, RUDD AND PERCH ON THE ROYAL CANAL AND THE RIVER INAGH

Most of the coarse fish species in Ireland were imported at some stage. Perch and pike probably arrived in the 16th and 17th centuries; carp during the reign of James I; whereas roach are fairly recent – probably appearing in late Victorian times. Tench and rudd are no exception. It is likely that tench came over with carp, or possibly earlier when they were imported from monastic stew ponds. The belief is that rudd came over with bream, possibly around the time of the Norman Conquest. All species have done very well, tench and rudd in particular. The clear, pure, rich waters produce great specimens, and the rudd do grow large. Two-pounders are common and the tench average a high weight, usually between four and six pounds. The colossal tench of the English gravel pit scene have not appeared but Ken Whelan in his excellent *Angler in Ireland* records a fish between eleven and twelve pounds from the river Suck.

Both species are spread thickly throughout the north and the south and it isn't difficult to find good sport in most localities. Once again, we turn to Charlie Stuart:

'Tench fishing is probably the most exciting and frustrating of all the branches of angling that I know of. When things go well, however, you just cannot pursue a more rewarding fish. Some of my favourite venues are the canals of the Irish midlands, places where I've spent many an evening and early morning stalking the species. There are so many stretches of these canals that have yet to be discovered. Truly there are places where no Irishman, let alone a visitor, has cast a bait. Let's look, though, at a few stretches along the **Royal Canal** that are worth particular mention and have a good track record. The first one is the canal on the Dublin side of Mullingar. This stretch flows along the side of the main road and the landmark to head for is Mary Lynch's pub and bed and breakfast – something of a draw for tench fishermen. Take a right turn at the pub and you travel alongside the canal for about half a mile. Every yard is teeming with fish. There are huge shoals of roach and rudd that can prove difficult in clear water. But it's the tench that are really special. In the summer of 2000 I witnessed huge numbers of tench and their spawning ritual. I tell you, this isn't a sight for the weak hearted. There were heaving masses of fish thrashing in the water, quite oblivious to my presence. It was pointless to take the rod out of the car, but what a beautiful sight to behold.

'As any good tench fisherman knows, the best times for the canal are from dawn until about ten in the morning, and then from around eight o'clock in the evening until it's too dark to see a float. The most successful method I have found is to use a common earthworm tipped with a single red or white maggot. I've fished alongside other anglers who have been using different baits, and whereas they've blanked, I've had a few good fish. Float fishing works very well indeed, and you won't be in any doubt when the tench are in your swim because they really bubble like crazy things here. Darkness and you pack up and make the short walk back to Mary's for a pint of the 'black stuff' and a wholesome supper. And then it's up to bed, in all probability your room being one of those that overlooks the canal itself. A fisherman's paradise.

'Another extremely good spot for tench fishing is **Lough Patrick** outside Multifarnham, located between Mullingar and Edgeworthstown. The lough is easy to find and locals will direct you. Boat hire is available in Multifarnham and I'd really advise a visit if you're intending to travel to the area. My one word of advice is to bring along plenty of ground bait even though the lake itself is quite small. The fish need a little tempting to bring on the feed but, once you've cracked it, the rewards are endless.

'It is almost impossible knowing where to start giving advice on rudd venues. Rudd are almost everywhere. Perhaps they're at their best in the big, clear loughs, but you'll also find them in the Shannon, in the backwaters especially, and also in some of the rivers. The **River Inagh** in County Clare and the **Owenavorragh River** in County Wexford offer good sport. Once again, I'd advise going back to Mary Lynch's for some of the best rudd fishing sport that Ireland can offer. You'd be amazed at the number and size of the rudd that you can see there. Just to give you an example, I stopped over briefly one afternoon a couple of years back and caught four rudd, which weighed in jointly at over seven pounds! Not bad for about twenty minutes' fishing.

'Before I go, I ought to say something about the perch in Ireland. Like rudd, tench and bream, they're pretty well everywhere and there are some cracking specimens. But here's a last little tip. This little pond in the Forest Park at **Donadea** in County Kildare was stocked by an enterprising individual some years ago and has since become a place that turns up some amazing fish considering the water is so small. It teems with roach and that is obviously why the perch grow so big. I myself have had them up to three and three-quarter pounds, and one large perch that I caught coughed up a half-digested roach. So I don't have to say any more about the staple diet of the fish here. It's a tremendous place to visit if you're on holiday in Dublin. The park lies about four miles outside the town of Clane ,which is only about twenty minutes drive from the city centre itself. The water is shallow and how I fish it is to bait heavily with maggots and work the roach up into a feeding frenzy. The big perch then move in and you can pick them up on lobworm or, inevitably, a small roach dead bait.'

❧ HIGHLY RECOMMENDED FISHERIES ❧

• *Lough Muck. A thirty-five-acre lake that is rarely fished, just outside Omagh. Only twelve pegs and fishing boats available for hire. It has pike, roach and perch. Contact Kenny Alcorn for day permits on 028 8224 2618.*
• *Clay Lake, Nr. Keady, County Armagh. A hundred and twenty acres. Pike, rudd and perch. Controlled by the Department of Agriculture.*

WHERE TO
SEA FSH
IN IRELAND

Sea-Fishing Sites in Ireland

NORTHERN IRELAND

REPUBLIC OF IRELAND

IRISH SEA

DONEGAL
LONDONDERRY
ANTRIM
TYRONE
SLIGO
MAYO
LEITRIM
MONAGHAN
ROSCOMMON
CAVAN
LOUTH
WESTMEATH
MEATH
GALWAY
OFFALY
DOWN
CLARE
WICKLOW
LIMERICK
TIPPERARY
CARLOW
KILKENNY
WEXFORD
KERRY
CORK
WATERFORD

Tory Island
Inishtrahull
Church Bay
Rathlin Island
Aran Island
Portrush
Portstewart
Ballycastle
Coleraine
Letterkenny
Ballybofey
Larne
Ballymena
Island Magee
Carrickfergus
Donegal
Omagh
Cookstown
Newtownabbey
Belfast Lough
Bangor
Donaghadee
Newtownards
Inishmurray
Bundoran
Enniskillen
Monaghan
Armagh
BELFAST
Strangford Lough
Portaferry
Inishkea North
Sligo
Keady
Newry
Castlewellan
Inishkea South
Ballina
Rostrevor
Duvillaun More
Knock Airport
Boyle
Cavan
Dundalk
Achill Island
Swinford
Ardee
Clogher Head
Clare Island
Clew Bay
Castlerea
Roscommon
Longford
Navan
Drogheda
Westport
Ballinrobe
Inishturk
Caher Island
Tuam
Mullingar
Lambay Island
Cliiden
Ballinasloe
Athlone
Edenderry
DUBLIN
Galway
Loughrea
Dun Laoghaire
Gorumna Island
Galway Bay
Naas
Bray
Greystones
Inishmore
Aran Islands
Portlaoise
Wicklow
Ennis
Carlow
Carrigaholt Bay
Kilrush
River Shannon
LIMERICK
Kilkenny
Scattery Island
Tralee Bay
Fenit
Tralee
Tipperary
Clonmel
Wexford
Smerwick Harbour
Ballyferriter
Gt. Blasket Island
Dingle
Castleisland
WATERFORD
Dingle Bay
Mallow
Fermoy
Tramore bay
Cahersiveen
Valentia Island
Waterville
Kenmare
Youghal
Scariff
Dursey Island
Bear Island
Bantry
Kinsale
Courtmacsherry
Clear Island

Nymphe Bank

N

> *As you know, John, I'm primarily a freshwater fisherman for anything that swims over here in Ireland – pike, trout, rudd, even bream and tench, and you'll find me there. But, like many Irishmen, I can't just ignore the quality of the sea fishing that's on offer. It's simply mind-blowing. What's more, you can enjoy a great deal of it using your normal freshwater gear, so you don't have to be involved in a vast amount of expense if you don't want to specialise too much. Mind you, if it's blue-fin tuna that you're thinking of pursuing, that's a different matter altogether! You're not going to land a creature of a 1,000 pounds – and they do grow that big – with freshwater gear are you? And another thing – the coasts of Ireland are simply stunning. You won't see more glorious scenery anywhere in Europe, or the world come to that. See you there!*

RICHIE JOHNSTON, IRISH ANGLER AND AUTHOR

Richie has been very much my guide when it comes to Irish sea fishing and, like all the Irish, he and his friends have proved an absolute fund of detailed knowledge.

For the sea angler, the coastline is awesome. It boasts endless variety and limitless potential. There is a wealth of treasure to be reaped, from the small, humble mackerel to the huge blue-fin tuna which has made an exciting return to the coast of Donegal. You'll find quaint little villages with welcoming olde-worlde pubs and guesthouses, so it is ideal for a family holiday, too. Get yourself over there and get exploring!

DUBLIN

There are many possibilities around Dublin itself, especially with pollack and wrasse. You can try Dalkey Island, which is only fifteen minutes by train from the centre of Dublin. Another possibility is the port of Dun Laoghaire, which offers good pollack and bass opportunities. It also provides pier fishing, with dabs and conger in the summer months. You'll find whiting, codling and coalfish coming in during the winter.

Moving a little way down the coast, you come to Greystones in County Wicklow. To get there, just take the N11 south out of Dublin. There's a little harbour in the village, but if you turn right you'll come to the beach. This used to be one of the centres of Irish cod fishing, but catches have faltered in recent years. The great thing about Greystones – and the reason why it is such a centre for competitions – is the huge amount and variety of fish in the area. You can fish it almost year round, with just a quiet period at the end of the winter. In the summer, codling, bass, coleys, pollack and sea trout all show well. Coleys and codling feature from autumn throughout the winter. All the usual baits succeed – peeler crab, lug, rag, mussels and sand eels. However, don't neglect spinning, especially when the sea is relatively clear. It's a cracking method for sea trout and bass, especially.

Sea trout can be fished all along the south coast, as well as huge shoals of mullet. These seek out any estuary or trickle of fresh water and sometimes you'll find vast shoals, but, as ever, they can be difficult to tempt.

ACCOMMODATION – phone the Tourist Board in Dublin on 00353 (0)1 6057700.

TACKLE SHOPS – contact Patrick Cleere in Dublin on 00353 (0)1 6777406.

BOAT HIRE – there are plenty of charter boats available in the area; for details, phone 00353 (0)404 68751.

CORK AND KINSALE

Cork City itself offers some great sport, both inside and outside the harbour. Kinsale, a little to the west, boasts a fine natural harbour and has been a famous Irish angling centre for many decades. Kinsale is a lovely town with a long-standing fishing history, offering five hotels, at least thirty guest houses and, apparently, over forty pubs and restaurants! So, although the town is small, it has a friendly atmosphere and there's a great deal for everyone to do. The Castle Park Marina fleet is extremely modern. High-speed boats (with a forty-mile offshore licence) mean that anglers can try out several different hot marks in a single day. There's deep water close into the town – twenty minutes or so – so huge amounts of time are not lost in travelling. There are big reefs and plenty of wrecks, including the *Lusitania*. The area offers just about every fish that swims the sea, including some very good blue shark fishing.

There are several forms of wrasse around the shores of the United Kingdom and Ireland. Here, however, I'm going to concentrate on ballan wrasse. They are perfect for the shore angler, especially in areas such as Ireland where there are huge expanses of rocky headland.

• *Ballan wrasse prefer quite shallow water – generally not deeper than forty feet. This means that they will come close inshore.*

• *They like plenty of rocks, boulders and weed. You'll find them in exposed areas – often where you would think they'd get a battering from the wind and swell.*

• *Look for them in the tightest, rockiest, snaggiest, least accessible places! But don't put yourself in any kind of danger.*

• *If you have access to a dinghy, you can often get a boat close inshore under steep rock overhangs where it would be otherwise impossible to fish. The dinghy angler will get the very best out of most rocky headlands.*

• *You can leger for wrasse, but the problem is that the bait will frequently roll into chasms between the rocks. This sometimes means that it is hidden and tackle losses can be very high.*

• *Fishing with a sliding float is a much better idea. Try using a big freshwater float, such as a large Avon or even a small pike float – this slides perfectly up and down the line. A drilled bullet will make it cock and take the bait down.*

• *It's generally unwise to use mainlines of much less than twelve- or fifteen-pound breaking strain. Ballans can grow to nearly ten pounds and they always live in rocky terrain. It's important, therefore, to hit them and hold them from potentially tackle-busting snags. You'll also need a rod that has plenty of backbone to exert the necessary power.*

• *Peeler crab is traditionally one of the great wrasse baits. Wrasse have sharp teeth in their mouth and even stronger teeth in their throat so that they can cope adequately with the toughest of foodstuffs.*

• *If you are using worm – and king rag are very good – try to thread as much of the worm as possible on to the hook bend and shank, leaving very little loose worm hanging off. This helps stop small wrasse shredding the bait completely.*

• *Always be aware of the safety angle. Make sure you know when the tide is going to be in and that you're not going to be marooned. Always look out for a good exit point. Make sure you have good non-slip soles to your boots. Go with a friend. Never take risks on rocky headlands.*

A little further west you come to the delightful village of Courtmacsherry, which has all the sea angler could want – along with a beautiful setting to boot. The reef fishing is superb, with some huge common skate in residence – fish to nearly 200 pounds have been caught. You can pick up conger from the pier, and mullet and tremendous bass and flounder off the beaches. It's a great place for the whole family – there's lots of exploring to be done and you can always have a bash at the mullet that throng the area around the pier. Try very small pieces of mackerel on a size ten, for example. You can actually watch the meat going down amongst them and free-line. Or you could use a small float. It's the sort of fishing that children adore.

⊢ **ACCOMMODATION** – try the Cork Tourist Information Centre on 00353 (0)21 4273251.

○ **TACKLE SHOPS** – contact the Cobh Angling Centre in Cork on 00353 (0)21 1813417 for tackle and for advice and contacts in the Cork area.

⬤ **BOAT HIRE** – ring the Cobh Angling Centre (see above). For information on blue shark fishing, contact the Castle Park Marina Centre on 00353 (0)21 774959. Also try Mark Gannon in Courtmacsherry on 00353 (0)23 46427; Mark is very much one of the local experts and offers both accommodation, charter-boat hire and unparalleled knowledge of the area.

CAHERSIVEEN – CO. KERRY

The south west is where everything really begins to take off. How about the little village of Cahersiveen in south-west Kerry? It's just north of the enchanting town of Waterville and is set in really beautiful countryside on the famous Ring of Kerry. It's an all-round sea-angling holiday destination. It's close to Valentia Island, but there is a myriad of small islands, rocks, jetties, harbours – perfect for shore fishing and boat fishing alike.

The boat fishing here is very well organised and productive. And there are lots of pollack to be caught close in. Cuckoo and ballan wrasse proliferate, along with plenty of mackerel. You'll find coley, ling, bull huss, haddock, cod, plaice and even skate and shark in the deeper water. What more could you possibly ask for? And if it's conger you fancy, try the pier after dark.

Shore fishing is brilliant. Fishing from the pier is great, but also try the road bridge and the old stone fort. Coonanna Harbour also offers a tremendous amount of opportunity for pollack, wrasse and dogfish. Check out the mullet and the very big bass. You will also find a lot of the shore fishing blissfully unexploited, as most of the locals tend to go out in boats. Be prepared to do a bit of exploring.

⊢ **ACCOMMODATION** – contact the Irish Tourist Board in London on 020 7493 3201; they have an exhaustive list of accommodation in the area. Highly recommended is the Reenard House Bed and Breakfast on 00353 (0)66 9472752 – a lovely place with great views.

○ ⬤ **TACKLE SHOPS AND BOAT HIRE** – as far as the fishing goes, the Anchor Bar is the centre for everything that goes on – bar, tackle shop, meeting place and charter-boat hire centre! Hugh Maguire on 00353 (0)66 9472049 can help with boat arrangements.

DINGLE AND TRALEE – CO. KERRY

Beautiful Dingle Bay can be found just to the north of Cahersiveen. One of the most popular places to fish from the shore here is Clogher Head, on the north side of the bay. To get there, follow the road out of Dingle for Smerwick Harbour. Drive through the village of Ballyferriter and carry on for a couple of miles. The cove is signposted. There's a headland about a mile away with a car-park overlooking the small beach. It's a really good rock-fishing venue, and the sandy cove itself can produce good sport at times. You'll pick up specimen wrasse and pollack from the rocks. There are also huss and conger eels. The sandy beach throws up flounder, dab, dogfish and plaice. It's a beautiful area, best fished from April through to October – fitting in nicely with the holiday season. Do take great care when you are fishing the rocks, and don't think of going down there if there's an onshore wind or a big swell – it could prove dangerous.

Moving up the coast again, we come to the popular Tralee Bay and the famous little fishing village of Fenit. Fenit is well sheltered, in common with many of the little ports in this fascinating part of the world. The boat fishing is spectacular. June to September is tremendous for skate and the shallow water inside Tralee Bay offers marvellous fishing for both tope and monkfish. May and June are peak times. It's common to use a rubby bag and a mackerel flapper as bait. If the wind is kind, you can travel far out, but if it's stormy, you can just tuck into the bay itself and enjoy some cracking sport there. The shore fishing is also superb. Monkfish are possible and the bass fishing is excellent. You can even, if you're lucky, pick up common skate from the pier. So, if boat fishing isn't for you, there are other possibilities!

⊢ ACCOMMODATION – in Dingle, contact the Tourist Information Centre on 00353 (0)66 9151188 or try the Pax House on 00353 (0)66 9151518. In Tralee, contact the Tourist Information Centre on 00353 (0)66 7121288 or try the Rosedale Lodge on 00353 (0)66 7125320. In Fenit, Godley's Hotel is the centre for everything – call 00353 (0)66 7136108.

○ TACKLE SHOPS – tackle can be bought at the Dingle Marina (see below).

⬤ BOAT HIRE – contact the Dingle Marina on 00353 (0)66 9151629.

KILRUSH – CO. CLARE

The Shannon estuary has some great possibilities, and the town of Kilrush is particularly popular. There's some superb pier fishing offering conger, flounder and dogfish. However, the shark-fishing possibilities are enormous and so it pays to consider getting afloat.

Kilrush certainly merits the support of sea anglers everywhere. Several million pounds have been spent on creating a lock system to trap the flow of the Shannon and to give access from the spanking new marina out on to the sea. What you have now at Kilrush is a safe base – even in the winter – on the exposed west coast of Ireland, along with the security and the facilities of a purpose-built marina.

The fishing is absolutely superb. There are plenty of tope, which provide great sport on lighter gear. Thornbacks proliferate, along with bull huss, common skate, conger and blue shark. There are endless well-known marks such as Scattery Island and Carrigaholt Bay. Excellent stuff.

⊢ **ACCOMMODATION** – Shannon Angling on 00353 (0)65 52031 offers both boat charter and accommodation.

○ **TACKLE SHOPS** – contact Michael O'Sullivan on 00353 (0)65 51071 or Michael Clancy on 00353 (0)65 51107.

⚓ **BOAT HIRE** – try Atlantic Adventures on 00353 (0)65 52133 or Shannon Angling (as above). The Kilrush Creek Marina on 00353 (0)65 52072 is the hub of everything.

CONNEMARA – CO. GALWAY

Moving up to Connemara, you can't do better than the town of Clifden – really picturesque, great bars, great scenery and some great fishing. There are really good possibilities for deep-sea shark fishing. Another excellent place is Westport, in the south-east corner of the famous Clew Bay. Clew Bay is sheltered by the wonderful Achill and Clare Islands. This is a huge bay dotted with some 300 tiny islands, so there's always shelter for those wanting to take a boat out.

The fishing is quite magnificent. Inside Clew Bay, you'll find ray, tope, skate and turbot. Move a little out of the bay and you'll come into the grounds of cod, pollack, coalfish and the occasional John Dory. You've got to go heavy for the skate hereabouts because they really grow large – it's wise to use fifty- to eighty-pound plus gear, with perhaps 8/0 hooks. Remember that it's illegal to kill skate and all must be tagged and returned. You can go a bit lighter for the tope fishing – thirty-pound class should suffice, with 6/0 hooks. You'll need a wire trace and a long leader of very heavy nylon. If tope begin to twist, then lighter lines can go with a vengeance.

Check out Tramore Bay, not a particularly well-marked place, but one that offers fantastic tope fishing, especially around Claggan Island. Tramore is attractive to tope because of the huge numbers of flatfish it contains. There are also mussel beds to the west, home to giant monkfish. Multiple catches of tope around Claggan Island are not unusual, with some big fish amongst them. The Central Fisheries Board has had a tagging operation in place for some time now, and catch and release is certainly the way forward.

Away from it all in the far west of Ireland, a fisherman enjoys what the country has to offer.

Fishing for sea trout in Ireland's estuaries is increasingly popular.

A scene at Delphi, County Galway.

Ranji, the Indian prince who loved to fish at Ballynahinch in County Galway.

The rugged Connemara coastline in County Galway.

Ballynahinch Castle in Galway, the spiritual home of Ranji. Salmon-fishing splendour.

The Moy at Ballina in County Mayo. Salmon fishing has become a spectator sport here.

Healy's Hotel, Pontoon, Foxford, County Mayo – one of the best anglers' bases in Ireland.

❋ FISHING FOR TOPE ❋

Tope are a free-running species, so you will get a tremendous all-action fight from them. Ireland is one of the really hot areas for tope fishing.

• *When you are fishing over a rugged reef or a place where there are snags or very strong currents, thirty- or even fifty-pound class tackle is advisable.*

• *If the water is shallow and sandy without big tidal pushes, very heavy freshwater gear will mostly suffice. Use heavy carp or pike rods, along with fifteen- or twenty-pound line.*

• *Mono is generally considered preferable to braid for tope fishing. The elasticity of mono, often considered a drawback in many forms of sea fishing, is actually good when you're pursuing very fast-swimming tope. Line stretch is often a blessing, especially for the inexperienced angler.*

• *Rigs: you needn't use more than twelve to eighteen inches of wire to cope with a tope's teeth. A few feet of heavy-duty nylon – sixty to 100 pounds – make up the leader. Hooks should be 6/0 or 8/0, depending on bait.*

• *Bait: a whole dead mackerel can produce big fish, but also use strips of the fish and try and leave the guts exposed. Cut off the tail of any dead fish to stop it twisting in the tide, looking suspicious and kinking the line. Calamari squid provide a really good alternative bait.*

• *Timing the strike: tope have often been thought of much like pike – they run, stop, turn the bait and then take it in. For this reason, tope angling in the past was often built around the longest delayed strike. This resulted in deep hooking and dead fish. Far better to hit a fish soon after the run develops. Timing is largely down to experience. Strike early with the first run and, if you miss, just delay a few seconds for the next and so on. A lost fish is better than a deeply hooked dead one.*

• *Play the fish calmly and with determination. Don't let the tope dominate the fight or it will simply tire itself out.*

• *Once in the boat, don't let a tope thrash about on the bottom. A carp-style unhooking mat is a very good idea here for the fish's welfare. Try to kneel over the fish so that it's between your legs – its head, obviously, pointing away from you. A T-bar disgorger is necessary to get beyond the teeth and to have enough grip to get the hook from the tough skin. Try to have somebody else keeping control of the tail.*

• *If you must take a photograph, make sure that you support the weight of its body cavity with your arm to avoid damaging the fish internally.*

• *Above all, get that fish back as quickly as possible. Tope are coming back big time; only our care for them will see this promising trend continue.*

This is excellent sport – the water is shallow and often clear with endless inlets and bays to explore. And in such skinny water, don't the fish go! Expect long runs and breathtaking fights, especially on light gear.

This part of Ireland is now easily accessible. Of course, you can still do the mammoth drive across England, ferry cross the Irish Sea and then drive the breadth of Ireland. Alternatively, you can fly into Knock Airport in no time at all.

⊨ ACCOMMODATION – for angler-friendly accommodation, contact Josephine and Mattie Geraghty on 00353 (0)97 85741.

⊷ BOAT HIRE – the area is well set up with enterprising skippers. Try Micky Lavelle on 00353 (0)97 85669. For deep-sea shark fishing, contact J. Brittain on 00353 (0)95 21073 or J. Ryan on 00353 (0)95 21069.

DONEGAL

Let's move north even further, up to the splendid county of Donegal. Downings is really beginning to make a reputation for itself, just inland from the famous Tory Island. There's tremendous shore fishing around here, with piers, rocks, estuaries and beaches. The pier offers conger, especially on a mackerel head at night. You'll also find flounder, plaice and dab. If you move westwards from the pier, you'll come across several rock marks. Expect thornback, ray, flatfish, pollack and mackerel – superb spinning opportunities during the summer.

Close by is the wonderful beach of Tra Na Rossan. This offers brilliant September and early October opportunities with bass. Try to the left of the beach, tight to the rocks – especially on the early flood tide. You'll pick up flatfish all the year, with plaice quite common from June through to October. Also expect thornback and spotted ray and a few turbot in the early autumn. Huss come close into those rocks at night.

Going back to Downings, it would be totally wrong not to mention the most exciting development of all, one that has all tongues wagging – the return of the blue-fin tuna, the so called 'tunny' that dominated the big game-fishing psyche back in the 1930s and 1940s. In those days, most of the fishing took place on the east coast of England, but the overfishing of mackerel shoals drove these monstrous, beautiful creatures away. Nowadays, however, there are signs that the coast of Donegal could be the new stamping ground for people wishing to test themselves against these spectacular fish.

Much of this has to do with the North Atlantic drift, which warms the coastal waters as it brushes the west coast of Ireland on its way to Scotland. The big fish follow their prey and come close in to the coast of Donegal. Mid-August is, arguably, the best time of all but the season does run much earlier and later. You're talking about big fish – certainly 300- and 400-pounders, but tuna of 500 to 1,000 pounds are always possible. For this reason, you must use heavy-duty gear. We're talking a 130-pound test

Ballynahinch Castle in Galway, the spiritual home of Ranji. Salmon-fishing splendour.

The Moy at Ballina in County Mayo. Salmon fishing has become a spectator sport here.

Healy's Hotel, Pontoon, Foxford, County Mayo – one of the best anglers' bases in Ireland.

Away from it all in the far west of Ireland, a fisherman enjoys what the country has to offer.

Fishing for sea trout in Ireland's estuaries is increasingly popular.

A scene at Delphi, County Galway.

Ranji, the Indian prince who loved to fish at Ballynahinch in County Galway.

The rugged Connemara coastline in County Galway.

❖ FISHING FOR TOPE ❖

Tope are a free-running species, so you will get a tremendous all-action fight from them. Ireland is one of the really hot areas for tope fishing.

• *When you are fishing over a rugged reef or a place where there are snags or very strong currents, thirty- or even fifty-pound class tackle is advisable.*

• *If the water is shallow and sandy without big tidal pushes, very heavy freshwater gear will mostly suffice. Use heavy carp or pike rods, along with fifteen- or twenty-pound line.*

• *Mono is generally considered preferable to braid for tope fishing. The elasticity of mono, often considered a drawback in many forms of sea fishing, is actually good when you're pursuing very fast-swimming tope. Line stretch is often a blessing, especially for the inexperienced angler.*

• *Rigs: you needn't use more than twelve to eighteen inches of wire to cope with a tope's teeth. A few feet of heavy-duty nylon – sixty to 100 pounds – make up the leader. Hooks should be 6/0 or 8/0, depending on bait.*

• *Bait: a whole dead mackerel can produce big fish, but also use strips of the fish and try and leave the guts exposed. Cut off the tail of any dead fish to stop it twisting in the tide, looking suspicious and kinking the line. Calamari squid provide a really good alternative bait.*

• *Timing the strike: tope have often been thought of much like pike – they run, stop, turn the bait and then take it in. For this reason, tope angling in the past was often built around the longest delayed strike. This resulted in deep hooking and dead fish. Far better to hit a fish soon after the run develops. Timing is largely down to experience. Strike early with the first run and, if you miss, just delay a few seconds for the next and so on. A lost fish is better than a deeply hooked dead one.*

• *Play the fish calmly and with determination. Don't let the tope dominate the fight or it will simply tire itself out.*

• *Once in the boat, don't let a tope thrash about on the bottom. A carp-style unhooking mat is a very good idea here for the fish's welfare. Try to kneel over the fish so that it's between your legs – its head, obviously, pointing away from you. A T-bar disgorger is necessary to get beyond the teeth and to have enough grip to get the hook from the tough skin. Try to have somebody else keeping control of the tail.*

• *If you must take a photograph, make sure that you support the weight of its body cavity with your arm to avoid damaging the fish internally.*

• *Above all, get that fish back as quickly as possible. Tope are coming back big time; only our care for them will see this promising trend continue.*

This is excellent sport – the water is shallow and often clear with endless inlets and bays to explore. And in such skinny water, don't the
fish go! Expect long runs and breathtaking fights, especially on light gear.

This part of Ireland is now easily accessible. Of course, you can still do the mammoth drive across England, ferry cross the Irish Sea and then drive the breadth of Ireland. Alternatively, you can fly into Knock Airport in no time at all.

⊨ **ACCOMMODATION** – for angler-friendly accommodation, contact Josephine and Mattie Geraghty on 00353 (0)97 85741.

⯈ **BOAT HIRE** – the area is well set up with enterprising skippers. Try Micky Lavelle on 00353 (0)97 85669. For deep-sea shark fishing, contact J. Brittain on 00353 (0)95 21073 or J. Ryan on 00353 (0)95 21069.

DONEGAL

Let's move north even further, up to the splendid county of Donegal. Downings is really beginning to make a reputation for itself, just inland from the famous Tory Island. There's tremendous shore fishing around here, with piers, rocks, estuaries and beaches. The pier offers conger, especially on a mackerel head at night. You'll also find flounder, plaice and dab. If you move westwards from the pier, you'll come across several rock marks. Expect thornback, ray, flatfish, pollack and mackerel – superb spinning opportunities during the summer.

Close by is the wonderful beach of Tra Na Rossan. This offers brilliant September and early October opportunities with bass. Try to the left of the beach, tight to the rocks – especially on the early flood tide. You'll pick up flatfish all the year, with plaice quite common from June through to October. Also expect thornback and spotted ray and a few turbot in the early autumn. Huss come close into those rocks at night.

Going back to Downings, it would be totally wrong not to mention the most exciting development of all, one that has all tongues wagging – the return of the blue-fin tuna, the so called 'tunny' that dominated the big game-fishing psyche back in the 1930s and 1940s. In those days, most of the fishing took place on the east coast of England, but the overfishing of mackerel shoals drove these monstrous, beautiful creatures away. Nowadays, however, there are signs that the coast of Donegal could be the new stamping ground for people wishing to test themselves against these spectacular fish.

Much of this has to do with the North Atlantic drift, which warms the coastal waters as it brushes the west coast of Ireland on its way to Scotland. The big fish follow their prey and come close in to the coast of Donegal. Mid-August is, arguably, the best time of all but the season does run much earlier and later. You're talking about big fish – certainly 300- and 400-pounders, but tuna of 500 to 1,000 pounds are always possible. For this reason, you must use heavy-duty gear. We're talking a 130-pound test with 16/0 hooks allied with 300- or even 400-pound traces. These fish battle brutally: they'll pick up your mackerel bait with a screaming run and then give a wonderful fight. They run long and hard, always pushing deeper. Okay, you won't see them tail-walking, but that doesn't take anything from the wonder of the fight. These are fish that just never give in.

What you don't really want – for your comfort as much as anything else – is stormy weather. You will often find these massive fish pretty close in, certainly within four or five miles of the shore. The mackerel are the key to finding them, being the major prey of the tuna shoals. Of course, you're never quite sure at what level the mackerel are running and where the fish will be feeding, though on some blessed occasions you will actually see the tuna hit into shoals of mackerel on the surface. Could there be a more exciting sight on the seas?

It's most common to use balloons as floats and set your baits – live mackerel – at differing depths. For example, work some on the surface, others at mid-water and others down deep; just off the bottom, in fact.

A preferred method is to use a live mackerel and troll it very slowly behind the boat. Be warned, you'll be in no doubt when a tuna is on – prepare for absolute fireworks.

Derek Noble is really the expert on tuna fishing in Ireland. He reckons that late August through to October is the very best time for these amazing fish. They probably hang on later than that, but weather, of course, is a major problem. It's taken Derek quite a long time to get to grips with the fish and, even though he was seeing them, it was a while before he began to experience hook-ups. Live mackerel are good, but artificials also can work well when, like Derek, you know what you're doing.

There's certainly no shortage of fish. Some of the groups are only five or six strong, but thirty to forty is probably more common. And, just occasionally, you will see hundreds, with areas of water twice the size of a football pitch just erupting with these big fish – and I mean big. The average size of the tuna that Derek is taking at the moment is something over 300 pounds – and that's nothing! In September 2001, he saw a colossal fish come out of the water about seventy yards away from his boat – a fish well over 400 pounds. This is really thrilling stuff and you don't necessarily have to hook into a fish to appreciate the day if you see one as close as this. As Derek says, to watch the sea-birds shear off the surface as these colossal fish plough through the waves is a sight never to be forgotten.

One thing that Derek stresses is a catch-and-release policy. It's important to do our bit for the future and although tuna can be valuable, it has to be taken in and iced as quickly as possible – not something you want to do if you're intent on enjoying a day's sport. So, put the monetary side right out of your mind and just enjoy one of the most incredible sport-fishing experiences in the world today. And we are fortunate enough to have it virtually on our doorstep!

ACCOMMODATION – contact the Tourist Information Office on 00353 (0)73 21148.

○ TACKLE SHOPS – try Erinn Tackle in nearby Ramelton on 00353 (0)872806607 for all the latest information.

🚢 BOAT HIRE – contact E. O'Callaghan on 00353 (0)73 31288, Brian McGilloway on 00353 (0)73 31144 or Antony Doherty on 00353 (0)73 31079.

PORTRUSH AND RATHLIN ISLAND

The availability of sea fishing in Northern Ireland has been promoted on a huge scale over the last few years. The Northern Irish Tourist Board has recognised that angling is a very important part of tourism in Ireland and has worked diligently to promote it. With excellent results, too – both on the fresh- and sea-water fronts. Southern Ireland often grabs the attention when it comes to all manner of fishing, but the north shouldn't be forgotten – certainly for sea fish. It boasts hundreds of miles of staggeringly beautiful coastline, unpolluted and unexploited. There are well over twenty species of sea fish regularly caught, including all the favourites such as bass, tope, shark and skate.

Portrush is a favourite area near the mouth of Lough Foyle and the River Bann. The town offers good pier and beach fishing and there are conger in the harbour itself.

Moving round the coast, we come to the magical Rathlin Island, situated a little way off the coast opposite the town of Ballycastle. This offers really good wreck fishing in Church Bay and some tremendous sport with just about everything.

⊢ ACCOMMODATION – contact the Tourist Information Centre in Portrush on 028 7082 3333.

○ TACKLE SHOPS – Joe Mullan is a mine of information; contact him at his tackle shop at 74 Main Street, Portrush, telephone 028 7082 2209.

🚢 BOAT HIRE – Geoff Farrow in Portstewart (close to Portrush) offers boats for hire – contact him on 01265 836622. Contact C. McCaughan on 01265 762074 for details about boats in the Rathlin Island area.

BANGOR AND DONAGHADEE – CO. DOWN

Just over ten miles from Belfast city itself, you'll find the town of Bangor situated on Belfast Lough. This lough offers some really sheltered, prolific fishing. You can dig your own lugworm and expect to catch good flatfish, along with codling and whiting in season. There are even some turbot.

Just south of Bangor, you will come to Donaghadee, which offers pier and rock fishing for pollack and codling and huge numbers of mackerel in the summer months. The Rigg sandbar is a good mark off shore, offering mixed sport.

⊢ ACCOMMODATION – contact the Tourist Information Centre in Bangor on 028 9127 0069.

○ TACKLE SHOPS – try Trap and Tackle on 01247 458515.

🚢 BOAT HIRE – contact Mr Nelson on 01247 883403 for wreck and reef fishing.

BRAID

As technology moves on, braid becomes ever more efficient, offering an alternative to nylon. It is perfect for signalling bites... the slightest tap bucks the rod over. With its reduced diameter it's excellent for holding deep water in strong tides with a minimum of lead. It's also limp and doesn't spook the fish, but there can be problems.

• Knots and braid haven't always gone well together, so obey any knotting instructions that come with the line. Use a doubled length of line for all knots. Dab superglue on the knots for added strength.

• Put the backing on the reel as tight as it will go to avoid bedding-in. Load the braid itself under pressure and not just from a free spool. This will probably require a friend to help out.

• Casting is easy with a fixed-spool reel, but not as straightforward with a multiplier. Presuming you are using a multiplier, don't go too fine or the spool's braking will cause a problem. If this is proving difficult consider using the new forms of coated braid, which can help.

• Start your cast with maximum braking force – for example, two big brake locks and the use of thick oil. Make sure your cast is smooth and not snatched.

• Use a longer shock leader than usual – say ten or twelve turns round the spool, at least.

• Braid comes into its own particularly when spinning or float fishing with a delicate rod and fixed-spool reel. Casting is enhanced, and there is less chance of breaking up on fine lines.

• Always check your braid very carefully for any evidence of wear and tear. It might seem indestructible, and often proves to be so when you're pulling for a break; however, when you go to unhook that elusive monster conger it can snap like cotton! If you're in any doubt, and you fear that the line may be fraying, then (expensive though it may be), re-spool and start again.

• Remember that not all braids are similar – there are many different types available. Experiment with the different brands until you find the make that best suits your purposes.

• My own opinion? I'm going to be controversial here: experience in many different types of water all over the world leads me to say that if you are fishing over particularly rocky and punishing ground then you are possibly better off considering ordinary nylon. In my experience, nylon is that little bit more resistant to the chafing that harsh ground gives it and is less likely to snap unexpectedly. Braid does have many advantages, but the measure of unpredictability in tough environments casts doubt over it in my mind.

STRANGFORD LOUGH – CO. DOWN

Strangford Lough offers some superb boat fishing and is sheltered from all but the very worst of the winds. There's excellent skate and tope fishing, but note that both fish are protected and must be returned alive. There's some very good wrasse around the entrance to the lough where the water is deep.

One of the beauties of sea fishing in Northern Ireland is that to some extent you are still something of a pioneer, even in the 21st century. Okay, the locals and some visitors in the know are well aware of the possibilities but even today the vast majority of visiting anglers still head for the south. This can be a mistake when you consider the big opportunities and the warm welcome that the north extends.

ACCOMMODATION – contact the Tourist Information Centre in Bangor on 028 9127 0069.

TACKLE SHOPS – contact Country Sports at nearby Newtownards on 01247 812585.

BOAT HIRE – charter boats are available in the nearby town of Portaferry – contact Mr Rogers on 01247 728297 for details.

Author's Acknowledgements

My thanks go to Richie Johnston as ever, Rob and Stephanie Maloney, Paul Harris, all at Irish Ferries, Patrick O'Flaherty and all involved with the Great Fishing Houses of Ireland. A special thank-you to Richard Keays, Dr Ken Whelan, Michael Shortt, David Overy and all at Belle Isle Castle.